Sitting on The Fence

Darren + Tatiana,

To explore the world and give back to it so beautifully is a deep purpose and a gift you both possess. Thank you for sharing your hearts with us all.

♡ Margarita

Praise

"Soul-stirring wonderment! Personal yet universal stories and wisdom about the mysteries and magnificence of love. *Sitting On The Fence* will move you deeply and exponentially expand your awareness of love and of loving."
~ *SARK, Author, Artist, Succulent Wild Woman www.PlanetSARK.com*

"*Sitting On The Fence*, a profound and courageous love story that makes you want to be better at love. This book serves as a beautiful reminder that love is a choice best made with your heart and not your head. Thank you Margarita for the inspiration to love more deeply and openly."
~ *Jaden Sterling, Award-Winning Best Selling Author, The Alchemy of True Success*

"A beautiful love story that will spark an inward journey down into your heart to explore the depths of love and connection."
~ *Sue Dumais, Author, Speaker, Intuitive Healer & Coach*

"Reading *Sitting On The Fence — How To Love Without Limits* feels like you're on a journey with a truth-telling close friend. This beautiful book walks with us down a path full of real-life reminders of our true nature and why we're all here. Love is at our core and it shows up in so many ways. Margarita has a special way of weaving her personal story with stories of others, so I can relate and learn. I definitely recommend this book and will keep referring to it as time goes on. I'll be picking out chapters and lessons to teach my young daughter."
~ *Jill Wesley, Speaker Coach & Strategist, Science + Soul of Speaking*

"Margarita takes us on a journey from the jungle of fear and trepidation to the paradise of love. Her honesty, wisdom and self-realization cut right to the core of the heart and what unconditional love is really all about. *Sitting On The Fence* will make you sit up and listen to the call of your soul. You will experience a deeper understanding of yourself."
~ *Carmelle Kemp, Speaker, Spiritual Teacher, Mystic & Medicine Woman*

Sitting on The Fence

How To Love Without Limits

MARGARITA ROMANO

Trailblazers™
PUBLISHING

CANADA

SITTING ON THE FENCE.
Copyright © 2018 by Margarita Romano.
All rights reserved.
For information, address Trailblazers Publishing
by emailing info@LeapZoneStrategies.com.

www.LeapZoneStrategies.com

Designed by LeapZone Strategies Inc.

ISBN: 978-1-9995359-0-2 (trade paperback)

Our books may be purchased in bulk for promotional, educational, or business use. Please contact Trailblazers Publishing at 1-833-763-9613 or by email at info@LeapZoneStrategies.com.

First Edition: October 2018

10 9 8 7 6 5 4 3 2 1

Dedicated to my Isabelle...

"I fell in love with her courage, her sincerity,
and her flaming self respect.
And it's these things I'd believe in,
even if the whole world indulged in wild suspicions
that she wasn't all she should be.
I love her and it is the beginning of everything."

~ F. Scott Fitzgerald

I wonder why me
When the world has so many
To write, love, and live.

\- MR \-

Contents

Acknowledgments

I have worked on this book all over the world. The people that have supported me, inspired me, encouraged me, and even picked up my pieces when I fell apart on this journey, are all over the world as well. It really does take a village.

First and foremost, this book would not be possible without you Isabelle, my partner in love, in life, in work, in play, and in growth. You inspire me daily and support me eternally and for that I am beyond grateful. I love you. To Lin, Susie, and Fraser my fellow creatives, who played with me at the beginning of it all with Love Matters, thank you. To Jer for helping me believe I could do this. I did it! Thank you! To Heather, Kate, and Spooner I thank you all for being there, encouraging me and celebrating with me when this book started its official journey. Can you believe it? To Mastin, Kelly, Pat, Lisa F., and all my Bali Scribe Tribe, thank you for witnessing me and holding space for me as I found my way. Forever in my heart the lot of you! To Patrick, Amanda, Mieke, Doug, John, Jean, Sylvie, and Lisa (aka Roomie) – thank you all for trusting me with your stories and hearts. I am so grateful. And Lesley, my soul sister, thank you for your story, your talent, your generosity, and your big beautiful heart. Love you so much and with you to the end sista! To Lisa O., Gillian, and Brenda thank you with all my heart for the time and support you gave me along the way. You ladies kept me going. Jaden, you kept me grounded on this journey and helped me become a manifesting machine. Thank you so much!

To Mom, Dad, Steven and my dear family, my friends, clients, and the indispensable LeapZone Team...your love, support, positive energy, and belief in me has no price and I would not be at this point today without you. Thank you! And last, but not least, my four-legged posse. My incredible dog, the late Pixel – buddy you were one of a kind, thank you for showing me the way. And my magical herd led by Cache, along with Powder, Kahlua, Willow, and Finlay – you beings are my light in the darkness. I experience true fulfillment every day because I get to partner with you. Thank you for the honor and for opening my heart. Always.

In love and gratitude,
Margarita

Love is simply love.

"Give to the world what you see missing from it. That's why you're here."

~ Mastin Kipp

have always had a connection with bringing love to tense situations. I was voted "peacemaker" in my high school senior year, and just a few years ago completed a personality test that divulged my strongest personality type as, you guessed it, peacemaker. It's safe to say that I have peacemaking in my DNA as it has stood the test of time. I have always successfully played the role - diffusing arguments between loved ones, between co-workers, hell even between strangers! I do not enjoy conflict and always encourage people to communicate from the heart. The importance I place on holding a loving space for people helps me dilute conflict for myself and for others, hopefully increasing joy in this world - even if it's one connection at a time.

In 2010, I needed to reset. I was not happy nor fulfilled with my work, which was disturbing as I was running a business I helped to create after a very satisfying year off. I felt dull, uninspired, and extremely disconnected from my life's purpose. In fact, I was so disconnected I didn't even know what my calling in life was anymore. So, after much deliberation mostly with myself, I took some time off and focused on me. I will go into this time of my life in more detail later in this book, however, what I want to share right now is that in this time off I connected with a process that allowed me to rekindle my passions - creative writing and horses. This process allowed me to reignite the love I hold within – the love I have always carried into every situation throughout my lifetime. That spark in turn brought clarity on my purpose to increase the level of awareness in today's world around unconditional love. It prepared me to pursue my life's work, to be fulfilled by my quest, and the desire to positively shift others in the process.

And so here I am today, on a mission that I serve through my writing as well as the heart work I facilitate in collaboration with horses. In an age of technology and instant gratification, my vision is to encourage people to get out of their heads and back into their hearts to rediscover and reconnect to a kinder, gentler approach to life - for themselves and the people around them. To open to the universal love that exists, a love we all carry within us and have access to, a love that provides us with a global language of communication.

The story I share in this book is about how my partner Isabelle and I came to be in the year of 1991 when we were young, impressionable students and frankly, completely unaware of what our futures had in store for us. We both had boyfriends at the time, were about to start university, and never expected what hit us like a ton of bricks - an unquestionable attraction;

a deep love and understanding of each other coupled with an undeniable desire to share our life journey together side by side.

When I first had the idea for this book, I couldn't quite pinpoint what type of book to write. A memoir? A biography? A self-help book? None of these felt completely right...and then it hit me. This book is simply a true story from the heart – of how Isabelle and I came to be – and I am using our story to share my realizations, learnings, and ideas about the power of love. Love comes from within and it is all-seeing. It is not "just an emotion" or something to rely on others to fulfill for us - **it is a state of being**. A big part of our internal make-up that allows us to connect and relate to people and things. At the heart of every one of us, we all want to be loved for who we are, and not judged or expected to be who we're not. If we commit to tapping into this love we all hold within us a little more, this world can be filled with so much more joy.

This is the time to feel fully confident about who you are showing up as in your life. A time to feel on fire and unstoppable. This book promises to help you examine your perception of love, expand your awareness of how you show up in your life, and explore your connection to love and deepen your fulfillment in your relationships. It is another piece towards my vision to increase awareness of the true essence of love, which is at the core of every type of relationship regardless of sexual orientation, culture, color, gender, or age. Love speaks without judgment, with no agenda other than connecting two life forces that have existed and evolved over time and space. Love sees all and loves anyway, because it understands that deep down we all desire the good in life - whether we realize it or not.

The story of Isabelle and I is a vessel to pursue this discussion. Hopefully, opening minds and hearts everywhere to move towards creating a future that holds less bullying, gay-bashing, shootings...fights, abuse, and war. The more we as a collective can focus on coming from a loving place, the more we have a chance to drive out the hate in this world.

I share our story mostly from just before we met to about two years into our relationship when we finally told family and friends that we were together - with additional excerpts throughout our relationship since that time. My goal with using our story as a basis for this book, is not necessarily to talk about same-sex relationships, but more to share what I have learned about love by embracing a same-sex relationship into my life. A life that unfolded to me the gift of truly loving people for people, whether man or woman. To love the soul within the body.

I didn't always know I was capable of falling in love with the soul within a person, regardless of gender. Before Isabelle and I were a couple, I had only dated boys and honestly enjoyed it. I never thought much more of it. In fact, at the vulnerable age of 17, a female server I worked with at a local pizzeria in my high school hometown declared she was "in love" with me. Followed by another moment at the very beginning of university, when a girl in my drawing class came right up to me and asked me out on a date. I couldn't believe it. In both situations I responded with an open, loving heart that although I could completely respect that they had feelings for me, I simply was not attracted to women in that way.

I admit I did wonder what these encounters meant. I am a firm believer in the unspoken rule that if you are presented with similar situations repeatedly...there is something to learn from these situations. I am an intuitive person and can feel in my gut when I am avoiding something I should really face head on...but this, this was beyond me. I was not lying to these women when I told them I was not attracted to them beyond friendship...yet it still felt like there was something more to this story.

Little did I know that several months earlier I had already briefly met a woman that would change my world completely. A woman so powerful that the Universe felt compelled to warn me she was coming my way through these two encounters. This woman was the storm that altered my life forever. Flipped my world upside down, removed me from anything stable and predictable, and threw me into adventure, spirit, and most of all **change**. All power, strength, and creativity wrapped up in a blond-haired, blue-eyed, no-filter warrior queen.

My relationship with Isabelle and the experience of facing the many joys and challenges of being in a same-sex relationship with a woman very much the opposite of me, has opened me up to really feeling and seeing all that love can be. The heart loves what the heart loves, whether we like the opposite sex or the same one. The gift that was given to me - to love a person regardless of gender – has nurtured in me the ability and the purpose to help people connect to the love within, the true essence of love that we all possess. Some Indigenous cultures use the term "Two Spirit" to identify a person having both a male and female spirit within them. They view this as a blessing by their Creator to see life through the eyes of both genders. I like the honouring and the simplicity - love is simply love.

This book is a ten-part journey into love. Ten chapters that reveal ten segments of my life - and the pivotal shifts that blossomed from them – profoundly forming my inner journey. As you read this book, I support and encourage you to tune into the universal gut instinct you are naturally born with and tap into the love you hold within - to truly feel how love can open your world. There will be things in this book you already know and others that may trigger certain realizations because you are ready to explore them. My perspective on love, of connecting with people as individuals, enables me to focus on love from an unbiased, all-seeing place - like I'm sitting on a fence and can see that the grass is green on both sides. I'm not saying that I know everything there is to know about love, far from it and I'm still learning every day, but if what I have to share so far gets even one person living with a little more love than before they read this book, then that is a shift worth writing for any day.

In addition to reading this book, I also invite you to download the *Sitting On The Fence Supplemental Workbook* at www.leapzonestrategies.com/fence-workbook designed to help you dive deeper into the inner workings of your life, through accompanying journaling exercises for all ten parts of this book. I also encourage you to like my Facebook page, Love Matters at www.facebook.com/lovemattersglobal - a place to visit for inspiration on love and positive perspectives on living.

The journey begins.

*"To care for someone can mean to
adore them, feed them, tend their wounds.
But care can also signify sorrow, as in
'bowed down by cares.' Or anxiety, as in
'Careful!' Or investment in an outcome,
as in 'Who cares?' The word love has
no such range of meaning:
It's pure acceptance."*

~ Martha Beck

One, two, one, two...my head drums along with every footprint I leave on the flat, earthy, wooden steps laid out like winding piano keys, lovingly placed to create this beautiful path home. Home for the next 28 days at least, is in Ubud, Bali - a tiny piece of heaven in Indonesia. I have come here on a spiritual writing retreat of sorts to create the first draft of this very book you are reading. A book about the journey of one person into love - love of self, love of a higher power, and love of others. On this warm night as I walk back to my room contemplating this incredible journey that lies ahead of me, I bump into a magical woman I just met a few hours earlier on my first day here. She spontaneously reminds me, "Hey, look at the moon!" and then promptly continues on her way.

Snapped out of my reverie, I turn around, look up and am faced with a bodaciously big and boldly bright full moon. There are wisps of clouds seductively passing in front of it, and as I stare on I decide this is the perfect moment to make a declaration, a promise to my soul. So, I stand tall, look around to make sure I am alone and not about to identify myself as the crazy one in the group, and I say aloud, "I let go of everything no longer serving me. I surrender to who I am meant to be and what that will bring. I am ready. I am ready to show up."

As soon as the words are out of my mouth the clouds completely clear and the moon shines the brightest light possible on me. And in that moment, I feel like it truly is for me. I feel seen by the Universe and it is letting me know - yes, you are ready. A symbol, to represent that this is in fact my time to shine. I want to take a photo to capture the moment, but as soon as I even have the thought, the darkest clouds come in and extinguish this cathartic moment. I guess some things are not meant to be captured, only experienced.

PART ONE

Stay open and be curious.

"It matters not who you love, where you love,
why you love, when you love or how you love,
it matters only that you love."

~ John Lennon

A s I walk down the upstairs hallway of the theatre building at Concordia University in June of 1991, I feel butterflies in my stomach. I approach the doorway to the room where the chairman of the theatre department is holding the orientation meeting for new Design for the Theatre students in the coming Fall semester. I am filled with excitement for what is to be and hold a little fear for the unknown. This is huge, this is university and I'm the first in my immediate family to attend, so it's a very big deal.

I enter the room and am faced with a very large table that accommodates the chairman at one end, and a sprinkling of disinterested students around the rest of the table, waiting for the meeting to begin. I sit down and take out my paperwork. I am nothing if not prepared. We are to choose our courses for first semester and I am taking this very seriously. My parents raised me to first and foremost be respectful. Period. To respect people and rules and treat everyone fairly and with kindness. So, to me this means doing my homework and reading up on all the classes to respect the chairman and his time at this meeting.

As I ruffle through my papers, in walks a spirited, smiling, blond-haired, blue-eyed girl that sits down like she owns the place. She overflows with confidence, and bubbles over with ease. She introduces herself as Isabelle to the chairman and greets the rest of us with a smile, and shortly thereafter the meeting begins.

An orientation meeting is exactly that, a meeting to orient the student. To provide information and help on selecting classes and to answer any questions. Things are moving along smoothly until Isabelle decides to ask her first question. Now, Concordia University is an English-speaking university in Montreal, Quebec, Canada. Quebec is the province in Canada with the most French-speaking people. Isabelle has decided to apply to Concordia because it is the only university at the time offering Design for the Theatre. If you haven't guessed it already, Isabelle is completely, totally, and utterly French.

And so it goes for the next 20 minutes of this orientation meeting - my head bounces back and forth like I am watching a ping pong match - Isabelle asks her questions in French and the chairman basically keeps turning around in circles in English trying to comprehend what this student is saying.

Suffice it to say, I am quite shy. For me to pipe up, interrupt, and say anything at all at this point in my life takes every ounce of courage I can muster. But I persevere and blurt out to Isabelle amidst her passionate fifth attempt at re-explaining her question, "Excusez moi, je suis bilingue. Est-ce que je peux t'aider?" This basically means, "Pardon me, I'm bilingual. May I help you?"

Man, am I ever not ready for what comes next - little shy, respectful girl that I am. I think if I was a turtle I'd not only be tightly tucked into my shell, but probably flipped over and completely ready to surrender to my fate.

Isabelle's head twirls around and stops dead in my direction. Her piercing blue eyes burn a hole right through me, her stare is SO intense. She takes a deep breath and says to me in French, "You mean to tell me you've been sitting here for 20 fuckin' minutes and are only speaking up now!!!"

Yep. That's our first encounter. Ironically, it demonstrates both our personalities at their polar opposite. I leave Concordia that day mostly frazzled, but also with a tiny spark of pride for having spoken up. Yes, I chose to speak up with a powerhouse energy in the room and that deserves a large pat on the back. At the same time, everything happens for a reason...

For the rest of that summer, I work as much as I can to save up money for first semester and I take a very exciting trip to New York City, before I am chained down to submitting papers, taking exams, and working on shows until the wee hours of the morning. Despite having so much to do and accomplish before school starts, every now and then I catch myself thinking of Isabelle and wondering what it will be like to see her again. Will she remember me? Will I run in the other direction from fear of being chastised in public again? Only time will tell.

School starts in September and the time finally comes when Isabelle and I meet again in one of our shared classes. The first time I see her, I am instantly filled with joy and a sense of security? What's that about I wonder? I feel like everything is as it should be, and I don't quite understand it, but I ride the wave of happiness. A spark spontaneously ignites between us as we connect for the first time upon our return to school and we need no introductions. We bring each other up-to-date on our lives and discuss pretty much everything right off the bat. Isabelle makes it quite easy for me to open up to her. It is almost like she ignores my shyness and just speaks right to me - and I respond.

We discover that we each recently left our boyfriends to begin university. I had been dating a guy for three months over the summer, and Isabelle left a relationship of three years. We don't think much of the coincidence and continue to the next subject in getting to know each other. And then the next, and the next.

In the first couple of months of that Fall semester, one of the things that initially bonds us together is that we both like two different guys named Paul in the theatre department. Our secret crushes on them, and me being bilingual and thus her full-time translator, allows our friendship to blossom quite naturally and quite quickly as well.

University life begins with such greatness. I am loving my program, I have made this unique new friend, and things come relatively easy to me. One day in theatre history class, Isabelle is so impressed with me as she stares in awe while I file my nails, listen to the teacher, translate what he is saying for her, and then even answer the teacher's question all at the same time.

"You are incredible!" she says, "How do you think so quickly? You can go into a library and find any book within a minute! I would be there all day!"

This brings a smile to my face and amazingly makes me want to come out of my shell a little more. Some people impress with muscles, I impress with skimming through numbers and letters at high speeds!

Isabelle and I become known around the theatre department as the "Dynamic Duo". We do everything together and kick ass. I can easily say we are the two most accountable, disciplined, and driven students in the first year of our program. But then again, we're in theatre, we are probably the only two who aren't sitting around getting high.

One night, our department is having a party and a classmate asks Isabelle if Maggie is going? Now, as I said before Isabelle is French Canadian and French Canadians are known for their extended hyphenated names such as Marie-Christine or Jean-Philippe. So, the concept of shortening a name into a nickname is very foreign to her. So much so that she gets frustrated when she finds herself constantly explaining to people at school that her brother's legal first name is Bobby and not Robert. It's quite funny to watch.

"Who is Maggie?" replies Isabelle.

Our classmate looks at her in disbelief and exclaims, "She's only your other half!"

Isabelle obviously has no idea at this point that Maggie is my nickname. To her, I am Margarita. And I like that. Maggie came about for me in high school, and really stuck. Even my entire family went from calling me Margaret to Maggie.

It's these little things that keep bringing us closer and closer together over our first semester. We feel like every day there is a new present we get to unwrap as we learn more about each other, our differences and similarities, our likes and dislikes. There is an eagerness and anticipation to seeing each other every morning as we're in constant curiosity for what comes next. University is hard - long hours, new subjects, classes, crews, and homework - and we are doing it all together and that makes everything seem possible.

We start having sleepovers, at her place and mine, to do our homework together while continuing to get to know each other. One night I sleep over at Isabelle's apartment, which she shares with three other roommates. Luckily, she has her own room and so we both sleep in the double futon that she has as a bed. That night I am drawn out of my sleep in the wee hours of the morning by Isabelle having a nightmare. The hair around her face is damp with sweat, she is crying in her sleep, and rocking back and forth in fear – she is so distraught.

My first reaction without really thinking about it, is to gently scoop her up and lay her right next to me in my arms. I slowly cradle her, and stroking her hair I say, "Everything is alright, I'm here."

As she awakes, she is sobbing and a little disoriented from it all. We speak for awhile and she shares, "I keep having this same dream of being chased. I am never caught, but always running for my life!"

As I hold her in my arms, and her body lays almost directly on top of mine, we deepen our bond that night in a different way. Seeing this strong, independent, and capable woman so vulnerable and trusting...I feel connected to her like I have never been before to another human being. Logically I know we are two young women, classmates in university, experiencing a time to explore, learn, try new things – and at the same time I cannot deny the feeling of this deep, intimate soul connection. My heart knows without question that this moment is truth, and in my head, as I lie there in the dark consoling this fragile version of this person I have only known for a few months, a single thought crosses my mind, "Uh-oh what's happening?"

And so, this is how the tale of my open heart begins. In a time of new experiences, I make curiosity my friend and discover great new things about love and life. What I will share with you now are my insights on love after first meeting Isabelle. Love isn't always in the package we think it will be, love can also be scary because it makes us face our true selves, and yet, love is strong and takes hold of us whether we're ready or not. It's these things I discover in my first semester of university.

1. Love is not always in the package we think it will be.

After meeting Isabelle, I become a firm believer that love takes charge - whether we want it to or not. We all have our own ideals of romantic love and even specifically what it should look like. Tall, dark, and handsome that protects us like a warrior and is gentle like a butterfly or glowing, beautiful, and blond that can hold her own and has the heart of an angel. At one point or another, we all have that ONE persona that we believe will complete us, enhance us, help us be the best we can be - that person who will love us like no other. And that person is out there, they just may or may not be in the package we imagine.

Sylvie Gilbert couldn't agree more. In March of 1996 at age 16, sitting in a car in her parents' driveway in a small town in Quebec, Sylvie had her first kiss with Etienne. She had always known Etienne, being from the same small town, but only really started hanging out as friends with him a couple of years earlier. They spent a lot of time together in and out of school as their friendship grew closer, and Etienne quickly learned that Sylvie had strict criteria of not dating boys at least an inch taller than her 5'9".

When the time came for Etienne to make his move, he didn't let that criteria stop him. On Valentine's Day that year when they were 16, he took all the courage he had in his 5'5½" body, gave her a card and said, "I know I'm risking our friendship, but I love you."

A short while later when Sylvie opened the card it held

one simple question, "Do you want to be my girlfriend?" with two checkboxes that said Yes and No. Sylvie's initial response was panic, for fear of losing their friendship and if she was to be brutally honest, for the fact that he was a little shy of her height requirement. She checked off No, listening to her fear, and met Etienne after a volleyball game to give him her answer. She admits that as soon as Etienne drove her home afterwards she knew she had made a mistake. He was someone she could do or say anything with - and wasn't that what love was all about? No judgment.

It took Sylvie a month to finally gather the courage to ask Etienne one day after yet another volleyball game, "I made a mistake, can I say yes?"

And he happily accepted of course, sitting in the car in her parents' driveway. Sylvie now realizes that her initial refusal to date him was due to her young age and inexperience at the time. She had never been in love before and needed to process what she was feeling versus the "ideal" she had formed in her mind. Seventeen years after that first kiss, they were married. A year and a half after that, their first son was born. And the kicker? Sylvie hasn't thought twice about Etienne's height in all those years.

Once we can move past the idea of an ideal package, making room for love to show up is the first step. God, the Universe - whichever higher power you believe in - will not give us anything we cannot handle. So, make room. Open to possibilities and opportunities. Go to that Tuesday night reading club or finally join that group of friends that goes out every Friday night. **Allowing** ourselves to be happy and doing the things we enjoy shows our higher power we are ready.

Making room also means trusting in ourselves and our higher power. Believing in our journey of fulfillment and having faith that what we need will show up. Love tends to come when we least expect it, and when it does it's because we're operating from a place of allowance, abundance, and trust instead of a place of fear and scarcity.

Focusing on opening our heart and our mind allows us to see and experience new things. Things that may lead us to the next level in our lives. Staying in our same day-to-day routine physically and mentally will not bring us different results. Happiness is embracing following our heart in some way and choosing that every day. It is not a destination. For those who feel there must be something more to life, more to love - try letting go of one ideal you are hanging onto in your life. A perfect job, the perfect mate. Soon your heart and your mind will begin to open and moreso every day as you let go. Start listening to what shows up for you because chances are you have needs that are not being met in your life the way it is right now - be it love, career, family, health, or spirituality. When we are living what we are meant to be living at our core, love flows from us and to us.

Connecting with our heart leads to following our gut. Letting our natural instinct guide us. Women are known to be quite in tune with their gut, their instinct, however every single person has it. Listening to it, and acting upon it, are the two steps

When we are living what
we are meant to be living
at our core, love flows
from us and to us.

needed to effect change in our lives.

Wouldn't it be nice if we could all be what our heart desires us to be and live our core purpose? The funny thing is we can! However, years of childhood conditioning and influences from people, places and society cloud this simplicity. It takes us away from our natural gifts and what originally sparks us even as children.

I remember telling my mother at about ten years old, "Mom, I am going to be a writer when I grow up."

Now, do I follow that dream and become a writer right out of high school? No. I get a Bachelors Degree in Fine Arts with a major in Design for the Theatre. I do that because that is where my interests are at the beginning of university and what I believe I want to pursue. I also take however, English Literature, Composition, Drama, and Poetry as most of my elective courses throughout my degree studies because deep down I am still carrying a torch for writing. At the time, I don't see that my desire to write never leaves me and is simply not surfacing in my decisions. It's only much later when I start my own branding firm that writing rises into my life full force.

It takes constant connection to our heart and our gut to continually live our purpose and stay connected to love. Children do this naturally. It takes remaining focused on our own desires and not letting the negativity of others seep in. Living our purpose means we are loving ourselves which allows us to become ready and capable to love others. And when we do decide to turn that love outward, we may be surprised at what comes back.

2. Love can be scary because it makes us face our true selves.

When love shows up in a package we really aren't expecting, our values get tested and so does our courage. It makes us re-evaluate everything we ever thought was truth. That tall, dark, and handsome man showed up as a confident French, blond-haired, blue-eyed woman? What???

Being kind to ourselves and allowing ourselves the time we need to process is important. This means taking the time needed to figure out the risks of our choices, assessing if we're ready for any outcome, and evaluating where following this path could lead us in our personal growth. These moments do show up in all our lives. The more space we create to listen and look for opportunities to show up, the more they do. Whether it be in love, in work, in family...the big questions show up to test us, to push us, to guide us. And it is our job to let ourselves give these questions the attention they deserve because they are what connect us to our true selves. Especially in love. Love is in all our DNA, it is something everyone needs to give themselves to survive whether we are aware of it or not. It is our source of being and our fuel to creativity.

Energetic Healer and Bodyworker Amanda Shay feels that people today often lack connection to the love within. To the source that holds and nurtures our true self, that one thing we are here to be in this world, and that unites us to everyone and everything else around us. When she works with a person she can feel when they are not connected to their true self.

"We are all always working towards aligning with our true self," says Amanda. "The more aligned a person is, the more vulnerable, wholehearted and joyful they become. The more disconnected a person is, the more they fear opening to possibilities. They do not want to be a failure, so they fear the unknown and avoid taking a leap of faith."

Amanda knows her purpose is to inspire people to act on who they are meant to be in life. It brings her joy to help people become more connected to love on a bigger level. "We are all loved," she says. "It doesn't matter what you look like or how you act. We are all going towards love - it's everywhere."

And it is everywhere because it is who we are individually and as a whole. We can even taste it! Ever heard the expression "cooked with love" to describe when you can feel the heart and soul the cook poured into the food upon tasting it? The love we hold within is what connects us and allows us to recognize the love within others.

Ask yourself, "What does love mean to me?"

I discovered love means a deep, intimate spiritual connection. A bond that ties me to a greater power. A bond that includes a sense of responsibility, a deep caring - whether for another person or for myself and the things that spark me in life. Brené Brown, author of *The Gifts of Imperfection: Let Go of Who You Think You're Supposed to Be and Embrace Who You Are* says, "We cultivate love when we allow our most vulnerable and powerful selves to be deeply seen and known, and when we honor the spiritual connection that grows from that offering with trust, respect, kindness and affection. Love is not something we give or get; it is something that we nurture and grow, a connection that can only be cultivated between two people when it exists within each one of them – we can only love others as much as we love ourselves. Shame, blame, disrespect, betrayal, and the withholding of affection damage the roots from which love grows. Love can only survive these injuries if they are acknowledged, healed and rare."

Thinking about what love means will raise questions and with patience and allowance, it will deliver answers as well. Ultimately it is up to each one of us to decide in the end what feels right. What will allow us to move forward without regret and own who we are by fully loving ourselves and our lives.

3. Love is strong and takes hold of us whether we're ready or not.

Love is the strongest positive emotion out there and when we decide to see it in our lives...watch out! It can bring joy, happiness, delirium even. It can also bring about some serious decision-making too.

When love requires us to face a situation that suggests we go against the norm of what is considered "acceptable" in our culture, following our gut and trusting our inner knowing will lead us home. Every time. Trust that you and only you can know what is best for you. We each have our journeys to experience and we are the only ones who can know what feels right and what feels wrong. We may look outward for the opinions of loved ones who know us, but do not get lost in them. They are great to provide perspective, but in the end, we are the ones who need to live with the decisions we make.

Fear will surface when dealing with major decisions, and that's okay. The awareness of fear and uncertainties is what really makes us think, and further requires us to tap into our inner knowing because the brain does not have all the answers. The brain wants to keep us safe, and love will challenge that and take us out of our comfort zone every now and then – and provide the opportunity for us to acknowledge fear, and not dwell in it. Love at its source feels pure, positive, and overflows with possibility. Enjoy the ride and indulge in it. Love feels good and to deprive ourselves of that feeling goes against why love exists - why we exist. There will always be reasons not to love someone or something - from ourselves, our family, our friends - but allowing ourselves the chance to explore anyway is the gem. It is the chance to discover what is in store for us when we fully surrender.

I continue to pursue my friendship with Isabelle after the nightmare scenario at the sleepover despite the fear it raises in me, because that night I experience an intimacy and an intensity that simply feels good. I let my heart and my gut instinct lead me.

I bump into her every weekday morning after that night on the city bus to get to campus, and every time I see her on that bus I think how serendipitous it is that we end up traveling together. Like two girls in high school, we talk non-stop from the moment I get on, until we're sitting in class. Every moment is lived and loved to the fullest.

PART TWO

Be in the present moment.

"If you have your full attention in the moment, you will see only love."

~ Deepak Chopra

Time flies by that first Fall semester, we have started the cold month of December, final exams are under way and Christmas is around the corner. Isabelle and I are beyond busy, taking classes, studying for exams, and working late night shifts of costume crew on all the third-year student performances. Life is full and so we head to my place to sleep because it is closer to campus. At this point, Isabelle and I are inseparable, attached at the hip people say.

I share an apartment with two other roommates – two great girls I met in high school. The apartment is large enough that we each have our own bedroom. My room faces the inner courtyard, quite romantic except for all the posters of Jean-Claude Van Damme kicking butt in the movie *Bloodsport* that are plastered all over my bedroom walls. Yes, I am a bit of a martial arts fan. At one point in time, my brother and I could recite most of the lines to Bruce Lee's *Enter the Dragon* movie, and I had religiously taken martial arts classes for the two years prior to starting university.

My room also consists of a dresser and one twin bed - kind of awkward for a sleepover, but we make do. I separate the mattress and the box spring and throw them both down on the floor side-by-side. We're exhausted so we switch off the lights, crash into bed, and are instantly carried off to la-la land.

It's the wee hours of the morning when I am stirred into consciousness. I open my eyes to notice the curtains are creating a lighting in my room that is a warm shade of purple - nice. I never noticed that before, but then again, I am usually sleeping at this hour. I realize Isabelle is yelling and kicking at the sheets and my heart leaps out of my chest - another nightmare! All I want to do is console her. Before I know it, I am gently grabbing her and bringing her to lie right on top of me. I just want her to stop struggling, to feel safe, to know that I am by her side and won't let go.

She slowly comes out of her deep anguish, it takes her a minute to realize that not only is she not home, but she's in my room - and with me. I stroke her hair and tell her everything is all right. She cries a little and says, "I'm so scared...and so exhausted of running."

As we share this intimacy, in this moment, she is a part of me and I am a part of her. It feels like we're in another realm of existence, one I have never been to before. My breath becomes deeper and my hips start to move ever so slightly against Isabelle's body that is firmly pressed to mine. In fact, it surprises me that I am moving at all. I don't remember telling my body to do that! And to my surprise that's all it takes.

Before I know it, Isabelle breathes in deeply, lets out an exhale long and slow, and tentatively starts to caress me. I am on fire. Her touch feels like a feather it's so gentle, and she's ready to recoil at any sign of resistance.

"I don't know what's happening, but I love you," she whispers softly into my ear.

Isabelle's bravery in that moment, and sharing her feelings in that way, only ignites my passion even more. As much as I want to however, I cannot seem to find my voice to respond, but my body does.

My body reacts to every touch, every move. My breathing becomes sporadic and tunes in to every sensation. A loud gasp escapes my lips, I am so wrapped up in the ecstasy of it all that I can barely keep my head on as I catapult into a rage of pleasure. I am distantly aware that I have roommates in the rooms next door, but mostly I am delirious with intense passion and filled with feelings I have never felt before.

The next day reality sets in. We both wake up after an incredible night and lie there in complete silence. You can hear the wheels turning in both our minds as we start to analyze, and well, basically ruin the purity and beauty of the moment we shared.

"It's okay if you want to date other people, we're in university, now is the time to experiment," says Isabelle.

I listen to her, immediately think that makes a whole ton of sense, and let her know I am on board. But wait, didn't she tell me she loves me?

Yes, but with everything that happened last night we haven't even kissed yet...what does that mean? So of course, it's just experimenting...I think.

The alternative is to think that it may be possible we're in love with each other, and that just feels too HUGE even if our connection is undeniable. And then back to thinking that "experimenting" is the best-case scenario.

After our morning processing, we go to school and are instantly immersed in busy-ness. By the weekend I have invited Isabelle to come up to my parents' place with me at the lake. Our awkward conversation the morning after that very special night, ended up with us deciding to continue with our friendship, business as usual. So here we go!

We arrive on a Friday night and I introduce her to my parents and my younger brother as my friend from school. I still have my own bedroom in their house, with a double bed that Isabelle and I are going to share...hmmm, no problem!

The evening goes smoothly, we have dinner as a family and shortly thereafter Isabelle and I go to bed. You can feel the tension under the sheets as we lie side-by-side, each on our own half of the bed. I know the thoughts that are running through my mind and they don't involve falling asleep. I get the distinct impression her mind is on the same thing. However, despite these lingering, very active thoughts we both turn around and go to sleep.

The next morning, we wake up and stay in bed. We are

practically high-fiving each other, so proud that we made it through the night platonically. We talk about many things and the bond that has always been between us is very much alive in the room. I think we are both relieved to feel its pulse. The last thing we both want is to have lost our connection because of one night of passion and exploration - mindblowing as it was.

Our conversation leads to some kidding around and somehow, we end up with our heads under the sheet. At that moment, the conversation goes silent. We stare at each other for a very long time in the muted light that is seeping through the cream-coloured sheet. I study every fleck in her big bright blue eyes and notice how her upper lip is thinner than the bottom one. She looks at me with so much love in her eyes, I can't help but feel precious and beautiful.

Under that sheet our breath goes from two rhythms to one. We are completely in sync and present. We are here now. Our stares continue to captivate each other and slowly, ever so slowly our faces come closer and closer together. Our eyes close and in the dark I can smell her sweet perfume. Wrapped up in our own little world, our noses begin to brush together. Gently we explore each other's faces with our own. My nose guides me across her cheek and up toward her forehead. She is so soft. She explores my face in return, brushing her lips against my ear and coming back again toward my cheek.

She hesitates, but only for a moment, and then continues her exploration across my cheek towards my mouth which is exhaling ever so steadily. She pulls her face millimetres away from mine and waits. There is so much desire in the air I can barely breathe. Then gently, like the fluttering wings of a butterfly, she brushes her lips against mine and I gasp in disbelief. Who knew something could feel so wonderful?

We continue to travel across each other's lips, light as a feather. I am amazed at how delicate two women can be together... soft, light, every move performed with intention. We stay that way for several minutes, connected by the slightest touch. I can feel we both want more and are deliciously lost in time all at once. As if on cue in the perfect moment, Isabelle's breath stops, her lips part and that is it...we are having our first kiss.

The next two weeks are fantastic. We go to school, do what is required of us to complete our first semester, and then rush back to my place as soon as we're done to lock ourselves in my bedroom. Don't get me wrong, some of that time we do spend doing homework and talking, but mostly we are, ummm, "experimenting".

Before we know it, Christmas is around the corner and we are discussing going home to our respective families because that's what students do for the holidays. So, we arrange to celebrate our own mini Christmas before we leave each other, and I choose a night when we can be alone in my apartment. My roommates and I have set up a tiny Christmas tree in the living room in the spirit of the season. Isabelle and I eat dinner and then retire to a blanket spread out on the living room floor with only the Christmas tree to light the room.

We lie there for a while chatting about how our first

semester in university unfolded, and what we plan to do during the holidays. We talk about the traditions our families have, and are giving each other a run down of our typical holiday schedule.

At this point we start to cuddle and the topic of our "friendship" comes up. The last few weeks have been the best of our lives, and we have been very careful not to discuss that delirium with each other because that's not what people who are "experimenting" do. But now, on this night, it's time to be brutally honest because we can both feel that things have become more than an experiment. We discuss how our connection, our love, was more than an experiment from the beginning.

"We've both only ever had boyfriends Isabelle, doesn't pursuing this freak you out?"

"Yes," Isabelle agrees.

"At the same time though, I am so sure that what I feel is genuine and pure – like nothing else I've ever felt." And then, I continue almost in a whisper, "Do you feel the same?"

"Yes," Isabelle agrees once again and wraps her arms around me.

We take a leap of faith that night and before leaving for Christmas mutually decide we are no longer keeping the option in place of seeing other people. We belong to each other now. And that feels right.

Being present is the biggest gift I receive at this point in my life. Focusing on now and not allowing worry to drive my decisions, helps me to really tune into what is going on for me when I am with Isabelle. It is what helps me to realize that we are so much more than an experiment.

The rest of part two of this book will explore how love and patience are found in the present moment, and how seeing love from the inside makes the outside irrelevant. When we are truly living from a place of love – love of self and others – nothing else matters. This state brings a clarity and a peace to living that carries us through the good times and the bad.

1. Love is in the present moment.

If we sit still long enough, we can tune into or tap into the love within ourselves anytime we are frustrated, lost in uncertainty, or simply feeling disconnected. It can start off small like focusing on the things we are grateful for, then move towards connecting to the love we have for others - our pets, children, family, and friends. The point is when we tune into the present moment love **will** meet us there. We have that pact with our higher power, so use it. Be the fuel that ignites love in your life.

Once we've created that connection to love, living in love is a beautiful state of being that brings clarity. It brings a sense of relativity and perspective; a reminder of just how big this world is and how we can so easily get lost in our own minutia. It brings an optimism to move forward one day at a time.

If we are having trouble finding the love that resides

within us, focus on the present moment – what is happening right now? Not yesterday and not tomorrow. Direct our attention to what's going on for us in this very minute - and let it go. Allowing ourselves the freedom to not be attached to anything, to not have to do anything for a few minutes, is a permission we need to grant ourselves. Everything on our todo lists will still be there waiting for us when we return to it. The difference with taking some time to ourselves every now and then, is we allow ourselves the opportunity to return to our tasks with a different attitude.

The thing I find most beautiful about love is that to feel it, we need to give it. To give love is to feel love and that includes giving love to ourselves. When we can receive our own love, and the love of others, while paying it forward through good and bad times - then we have become love.

2. Patience also comes from living in the present.

There is a lot to be said about living in the present. You have just read about finding love in the present moment. Another thing that can be found in the present moment is patience.

Being patient with ourselves and our emotions is part of self love. When facing major challenges or decisions, and throw in biological shifts as we age, it can get very confusing - even frustrating at times. Giving ourselves the time and space to ponder, question, and feel what is right for us right now is being kind to our own needs. Patience is that time and space we allow ourselves, especially when our emotions are running high and our world feels like it is turned upside down. Getting angry with ourselves, coupled with negative self talk, will only amplify the intensity of our situation. Embrace patience and allow that connection to love to guide us through our emotions with much more ease and grace.

Fully living through our feelings is so important to our growth. Most people like to push their feelings down, thinking they can bypass potential hurt, sadness, or anger and move forward somehow leaving that emotion behind. This never works. Emotion needs to be processed by the body and the mind. Trying not to feel only delays the process and often builds on the emotion as it festers. Feeling our emotions, and most importantly loving ourselves through processing them, is granting ourselves the courtesy of gentleness. Nowhere is it written that we need to punish ourselves daily to survive and being kind to ourselves allows us the time to feel those emerging emotions and release them.

Doug Stimson knows all too well that daily self-punishment does not bring happiness. Up until the age of 25, Doug simply did not drink alcohol. He witnessed the harsh reality of alcoholism in his family and saw firsthand the results that drinking created. His mother kept no alcohol in the house, his friends didn't drink, and so Doug never picked up a glass.

And then he turned 25 and his circle of friends expanded, and he decided he would drink socially. No big deal, he had it all under control. Until he didn't. Doug ended up in a relationship that he didn't value nor feel valued in - and that drove him to

Allowing ourselves
the freedom to not be
attached to anything, to
not have to do anything
for a few minutes, is a
permission we need to
grant ourselves.

drink more. As the drinking increased he became promiscuous and eventually would come home drunk every night. It only took five years for him to progress from drinking socially to drinking with addiction.

Doug did not like where he stood. He too easily saw where he was headed in his father, and then again in his brothers. One night he came home so drunk he couldn't even crawl up the stairs. The next morning made him take a good, hard look at himself and with serious thought he said, "This isn't right."

He then proceeded to make a commitment to himself that he would never pick up a drink or even another cigarette again. And with his stubborn streak in hand, and an endless supply of patience, Doug has done exactly that. Today he is in his seventies and has not ever picked up a drink or a cigarette since that memorable morning many decades ago, and never plans to - because the decision he made all those years previous was for him. It was his way of committing to loving himself above all else, and that's why it worked.

It is crucial to remember not to judge where our heart is taking us. Doug didn't wallow in self-pity, didn't beat himself down until he no longer had any strength to take action. He made a decision and then moved forward - and in doing that he honored himself.

If our heart, not our head, starts to take us places that will potentially stir trouble and uproot our life as we know it, we need to allow ourselves the chance to go there. We owe ourselves the opportunity to explore, learn, and grow. We always have the power to choose our life direction, and providing ourselves the space to explore physically, mentally, emotionally, and/or spiritually without judgment, helps us to find out what we really want in life. Isabelle and I frame our exploration as "experimenting", allowing ourselves to feel without judgment, to find out if what we have together is real.

3. Seeing love from the inside makes the outside irrelevant.

When we live from a place of love, we see that beauty resides inside everyone and everything. The more we love, the more we realize that what is important, what feeds our need as humans to connect, is sharing in what people carry on the inside. We don't connect with someone because they have great hair, a great smile, or a beautiful smell - that is attraction. We connect with someone because we have similar beliefs, we share core values and truths, we tune into something deeper. We tune into love. Love is developed between two beings from this symbiotic connection along with a deep sense of caring, and that bond only gets stronger and stronger over time.

When there is a new bond of love created, a lightness forms between two people. I like to describe this lightness as pure joy. In the beginning of a love bond, everything is new, and we don't allow ourselves to get caught up in petty arguments and hurtful actions because joy overrules all negativity. That is a beautiful time to experience because we are truly **letting love exist**. Love is not being overshadowed by judgment and fear and potentially jealousy.

In those times, love creates a state of inner joy. If we can guide ourselves to tune into love daily - to live from a loving place every day - we can achieve that inner state of joy most of the time. I know this may sound a little "peace and love", and I am not suggesting that we can live in joy ALL the time, but we can learn to lessen the triggers that take us out of joy and return to it more easily.

Isabelle and I individually take the time, love, and patience we need to mutually decide that we believe in us and trust our love. It takes a lot more time, love, and patience however to get ourselves to that same level of belief when it comes to sharing our love and inner state of joy with our world. As a result, we discover that when love is caged, hurdles do appear to help break us free.

PART THREE

Trust yourself to show up.

"*Trust thyself: every heart vibrates to that iron string.*"

~ *Ralph Waldo Emerson*

After our mutual declaration of exclusivity, we each go our separate ways to spend Christmas with our families. We tell each other spending this Christmas apart is acceptable because we are nowhere near ready to share our profound news with anyone, especially family. We have barely had the time to digest it ourselves.

Since our unforgettable first kiss, we both keep a journal to write to each other when we are not together. During this first Christmas apart, these journals are on full time duty. A few days after my arrival at my parents' home, one entry I make to Isabelle is the lyrics to a song by one of my favorite bands - Depeche Mode. These words... *"I want somebody who cares for me passionately, with every thought and with every breath. Someone who'll help me see things in a different light, all the things I detest I will almost like."* Depeche Mode was tapped right into the middle of my heart when they created this song! Their lyrics help me realize that the intense feelings I'm experiencing, the same ones that make me so happy are also capable of making me feel so sad. I want to share our love and happiness with the world, but so many reasons exist for me not to utter a sound. To reveal our soul connection means taking the risk of losing all family and friends, potentially losing our jobs that help us get through school, and isolating ourselves from everyone and everything we know and love. Feels like a lot to lose simply for being two women...yet, reason enough to want to keep our relationship a secret, for now.

In addition to the journals, we also end up speaking on the phone every single day. By the time Christmas Day finally arrives, we can't stand it any longer. Isabelle decides to leave her family at a gathering held at her grandparents' home to drive the five hours to my parents' place to find me. I am ecstatic, my parents think it a little strange, but welcome her with open arms. Isabelle's mother however, is NOT impressed. Not in the least. She does not understand why her daughter feels the need to leave at this exact moment when family is gathered for Christmas. Her lack of clarity on the situation is understandable, but unfortunately, we are not ready to shed some light on our relationship for her at this time.

That night I await Isabelle's arrival. There is a magical snowstorm happening, and in the spirit of magic and romance, I decide to meet her at the highway off-ramp to escort her through the winding roads that lead to my childhood home located in the mountains on a lake. And more to the point, I cannot wait for our passionate embrace under the snowflakes upon our reunion. Funny how when you're in love, one week can feel like five years.

I wasn't counting on my 15-year-old brother Steven to be excited about having anything out of the ordinary happen in this quiet, rural area, and coming along for the ride. Considering no one knows about Isabelle and me, this situation is seriously going to affect our "reunion". As I look at my brother, one of the kindest human beings I know, I smile and say to him, "Let's go!" After all, I can't fault him for not knowing any more than what I've shared with him to this point.

As we wait for Isabelle to arrive in her small, white Renault 5 Le Car, the snow gently tumbles down and covers the ground in a fluffy, white blanket. It is extremely romantic. The flakes are so large they look like paper cutouts. I am so far gone in my thoughts...imagining Isabelle jumping out of her barely stopped car, and me running towards her in the falling snow, and finally landing in an embrace and..."Maggie, I think she's here!" says Steven - and I am abruptly pulled back to reality.

Isabelle and I run out of our cars and into a very long, airtight hug together. I am struggling to breathe, that is how much she is squeezing me. We stare at each other for several minutes, soaking in every inch, every breath, and telling each other in silence just how much we love one another. My brother waits patiently in the car and I finally return to lead the way home.

For two years after that we don't tell a soul about our relationship. Not one. We spend those years completely in love, but no one knows we are together. We barely understand the emotions we are feeling; how can we expect to understand the consequences of sharing them with others? We continue to write to each other in our journals when we are apart, in complete disbelief that we're feeling the things we are feeling...and it keeps getting better and better. Another journal entry to Isabelle describes just how much she has become a part of me:

I am sitting by candlelight now, just thinking of you and how much I can't wait to hear your voice again. Thank God for this little book - and the invention of a telephone, otherwise I would go crazier than I am now. Isabelle the day I see you again will be the happiest day of my life. I miss you terribly and want to see you with an overwhelming greatness. It's driving me crazy this distance between us. Everything I do or see reminds me constantly of you. All I see are those sparkling blue eyes peering over those slowly deteriorating glasses. And that mouth with no upper lip. It makes me laugh. Not because it's ugly, but because it is so cute. I wear your ring faithfully and cuddle your teddy bear non-stop.

We are on fire for each other and there are not enough words, songs, art, or colors to express what has taken us over. We're busting with so much energy that one night there is literally an explosion!

I decide to place a bottle of Baby Duck (cheap bubbly

perfectly priced for students) in between two windows in my bedroom for later that evening. It's cold outside and my roommates won't question the bottle like they would if it was in the fridge. Isabelle and I end up forgetting about the bottle and go to sleep. In the middle of the night we hear the loudest gun shot, fly out of bed, and almost hang from the ceiling in panic.

When we realize the bottle of bubbly exploded from the cold temperatures and is now a very pretty pink slush in my window, we burst out laughing hysterically. Non-stop. Her and I, in the middle of the night on my single bed split in two. It is the perfect symbolism to the explosive connection between us. The window not breaking from the explosion, my roommates and neighbours not waking up and calling the cops...makes it all feel like a beautiful sign from the Universe to trust the love that surrounds us and that we create together.

We are so in love we catch ourselves doing things that are completely out of character. For instance, in all her years at school so far, Isabelle cut class a grand total of one time - she is that disciplined and mostly, never wants to miss anything. On that special day she finally decided to skip a class, she found out later that same day that she didn't even successfully do it. Apparently when the students arrived for class, there was a note on the door announcing that class was cancelled! Upon hearing this news, Isabelle couldn't help but grin at the fact that she didn't miss anything after all.

One day we decide to successfully cut class together to go back to my apartment for a "quickie". The apartment is usually empty now as everyone has class, however, little do we know that one of my roommates is actually home.

We run into my apartment, go straight for my bedroom, and shut the door. We immediately begin kissing like it's going out of style. We bump into furniture as we try to kiss and walk toward the bed at the same time, which results in Isabelle jabbing my upper lip with her front teeth. We simply laugh as we are together in this sacred space and nothing else matters.

Just as Isabelle and I land on the bed and are fumbling to get our tops off, my bedroom door flies open and in walks my roommate, slow and steady, holding a butcher's knife in the air. Luckily, it's quite dark in the room so she must flick on the light to see what she is about to attack. This gives Isabelle and I just enough time to separate and pull our shirts back down, while screaming from surprise and sheer adrenaline.

"Oh my God, you scared me!" says my roommate. "I thought you were burglars!"

Scared her? We may be hiding from everyone, but she's the one still standing at my doorway holding a knife. She continues, "What are you doing home anyway, don't you have class right now?"

Very good question, I thought.

"Ummm, yes we do," I say, "but we need to catch up on some stuff, so we decided to skip class." It isn't a complete lie, we do have some major needs that require attention.

And with that she says, "Well, I'm glad it's you two and not complete strangers," and turns around and leaves the room.

Isabelle and I stare at each other, stunned by the recent events, and slowly let out a big sigh of relief that our relationship is still safe. Why do we feel like no one can know about us when being together feels so good? It isn't fair. Needless to say, Isabelle never tries to cut class again.

We are finally moving in together after the first year of university comes to an end. Waiting to finish our semester before living together feels like an eternity, but we both have leases for the year and now they are done. Moving day arrives and we float on a cloud. Even though we are moving into a third floor apartment of a three-storey walk-up in the student ghetto, to us it's a palace. Our palace.

We rent a three-bedroom apartment. As we are both in Design for the Theatre, we convert one bedroom into an office of sorts, with two drafting tables, an easel, and a computer that is good enough to basically teach Isabelle how to type. Despite this, we create a space that holds pretty much everything we need to build our creations.

The other two bedrooms are assigned to be exactly that - bedrooms. Even though Isabelle and I share a bedroom, to the rest of the world that second bedroom is "Maggie's room". We really don't like misleading people in that way, but this is how it must be until we are ready to share with family and friends that we are a couple.

It's devastating to feel this way. If we were a man and a woman I know we would very likely feel secure and excited to share our happiness and love while it's new and fresh, but instead we feel a need to recluse. The fear of rejection, disappointment, loss, isolation is huge - and therefore, we are taking our time to be absolutely sure about our relationship before risking the important relationships in our lives.

And so, for now, we wake up every day and live two versions of our lives. We even create our own word that means "I love you", so that we can tell each other in public. As a teenager, in the summer Isabelle would go live with a family in Toronto to help them with their children. The mother is Thai and the father Iranian. Isabelle would often see the mother embrace her children and say something that sounded like "nioika". She experienced that as such a loving moment that "nioika" becomes our word. To this day we're still not sure what that term of endearment means, or how to even spell it, but we know what it means to us and that's all that matters.

This cocooning of our relationship however, starts to take its toll. Even though we are completely in love and can't believe we have found each other, outside forces begin to create turmoil on the inside. Being in university, we attend our fair share of parties, and at these parties the young men make advances because we portray being single. Even though we know in our heart of hearts that we belong to each other and these advances lead nowhere, they begin to fertilize tension and jealousy. Disputes and arguments become increasingly common between us, and always revolve around our interactions with each other and other people. We become more insecure in our relationship the longer we keep it a secret. It is time for things to change.

The more deeply involved I become with Isabelle, the more I am asked to trust. Trust myself, trust Isabelle, trust the people in my life who love me, and trust that everything will unfold for the highest good. What I learn at this point in my life, and what I will share here, is when we follow our heart and turn love inward, we are truly supported to show up authentically and given the strength to successfully live our purpose. Love is about showing up in life as we are meant to be - and standing up for ourselves when life calls for it. If we are truly following our heart, we are ready for any consequence, and trusting ourselves and that we will stand up for what we believe and want in life, gives us the confidence we need to move forward no matter what the outcome.

1. Love is about showing up in life as we are meant to be – and standing up for ourselves when life calls for it.

Fully showing up in life means living from the heart. In other words, connecting to ourselves and others through the heart AND following up with action. Showing up is the ultimate way to love ourselves because it means we are tuning into our desires and allowing ourselves to be happy. When we allow ourselves to be happy we become clear on what we want and don't want, and what we'll do to get it and preserve it - and that allows us to clearly convey it to others.

Successful comic artist and comic book publisher Patrick Fillion started drawing at three years old. As a child, he remembers being most content sitting at a table with some paper and crayons. He also developed a passion for superheroes and would continuously draw his favorites. At the age of 12 he created his own first superhero and started writing accompanying scripts to eventually produce his very own first comic book.

Patrick suffered through the misfortune of being bullied most of his elementary and high school life. Music and drawing went hand-in-hand for Patrick and so often he would seclude himself and listen to music, while drawing, which fueled his inspiration. In grade 11 he entered a singing talent show at school. He loved to sing along to music, and coupled with a standing ovation he received at a previous family-and-friend oriented talent show, he gathered the confidence to face his bullies and his school. His performance floored everyone including himself as he realized that he wasn't inhibited, introverted, and awkward when he performed. He appreciated being acknowledged in a positive light by his peers and with every performance moving forward he increased his self love and confidence. He pursued music for several years after that, wrote and recorded two albums and performed across Canada. The more he performed, the more he grew into himself and the introvert that was bullied on a daily basis got further and further away. All the while however, he would continue to draw his characters at home to help him release stress and re-focus on whatever he had going on in his life. His paper, pencils, and inking pens were never too far away.

In his early 20's his music career started to take off, but he couldn't shake the constant desire to want to draw. He loved the feeling of being on stage, but he also longed for the quiet recluse of getting lost in his characters' lives at the drawing table. He searched within himself high and low, contemplating both music and drawing, connecting with how both of them made him feel. He realized that he feels whole when he is drawing his characters. He feels as superhero-ish as the characters themselves, and most of all his love for drawing is unconditional. He decided to let music go, and as soon as he did his drawing career naturally went to the next level. Today he and his partner publish over 30 titles and work with artists all over the world. Patrick still personally draws and writes the storylines to several publications that are close to his heart.

Singing allowed him to grow as a person and let go of things from high school that didn't serve him. Drawing allows him to learn about himself and share his soul with the world - every single day.

When we connect to our heart at the level Patrick did to grow and evolve, we naturally create a force within us that will stand up for what it is we want, or believe in. Loving ourselves also means building the strength to stand up for our values and decisions.

Once we connect to our heart and build an inner strength, we then need to have confidence in our choices when facing the important people in our lives. It is so easy to get scared and not end up following through on our actions for fear of hurting people or possibly pissing them off.

Isabelle and I listened to our hearts by choosing to be together and became stronger every day in our relationship as a result. It does take us two years however, to build enough confidence to stand up for our decision. To be able to face any consequence, to the point of potentially losing our family and friends once we share our news. This is not something to be taken lightly. In the two years we take to build our confidence, there are moments when we seriously wonder if all the upheaval that is sure to come in our lives will be worth it - this is fear talking.

Instead of giving into fear we decide to love each other through it. Loving ourselves, and others, through times of doubt eventually leads to clarity because we are taking the time to process the emotions that arise around decisions in the positive, safe space love provides.

2. If we are truly following our heart, we are ready for any consequence.

Ultimately, we all know what is right for ourselves. If we come from the heart, we will always find the strength to deal with any consequence that may occur. Isabelle and I wait two years to share our story with family and friends, but in reality, had it gotten out before that, we would have found the courage, strength, and confidence to stick together and face the consequences - one day at a time.

Loving ourselves also
means building the
strength to stand up
for our values and
decisions.

Often, we think we don't know what the right path is for ourselves, but if we take the time to slow things down and question and dig, we always know what is right for us. Our heart holds the answers, and if we quiet our mind to listen to our heart and stop our mind from trying to drive all the time, we feel less unsure and lost. Loving ourselves helps to create an inner strength and deeper connection to our core.

At 23 years old, Lesley Marlo was in love. She was in a new relationship, enjoying all the happiness and delirium young love brings, and was not expecting to need to get so serious, so fast.

Lesley found out she was pregnant. Boom - and there it was. She was carrying the child of a man, a boy really, who was nowhere near ready for this level of commitment and responsibility. The truth was she did not want to be pregnant in this way. In fact, she hadn't even begun to think about having a child.

When she confided her truth to a close friend, the friend steadfastly advised Lesley that if she chose to see this pregnancy through and raised the child, Lesley needed to go in knowing that it would without question be her own responsibility, and no one else's.

Lesley went to bed that night with a very full head and a very heavy heart...she bounced back and forth between the shoulds and should nots, and before falling asleep placed her trust in her heart and that it would lead her to the right decision.

The next morning Lesley woke up feeling like a miracle

had happened overnight. For what she was feeling within was unmistakably a feeling of certainty. She had no doubt that this child was to be born. And she hung on to that feeling to guide the way through her pregnancy after she had shared the news with the father-to-be. Initially, they remained a couple, however when he saw he couldn't shake Lesley's inner peace anymore, he turned his attention elsewhere and ensured his behavior made it that there was no other choice but to end their relationship. Lesley now had someone else to protect and that made her life decisions suddenly very clear.

As soon as Lesley gave birth to her baby girl, she knew she had just been delivered the greatest gift of her life. When she was nursing, she felt like her baby was looking at her thinking, "You don't know what you're doing, do you?"

Lesley thought, "No, but we'll figure it out together." And they have figured it out ever since. When we are clear on what we want, fear no longer wins. It becomes paralyzed by our desire to follow our heart.

3. Trust in ourselves.

The inner strength that loving ourselves creates is something powerful we can trust. It is a direct link to our capabilities and our dreams - the stuff that drives us towards living our purpose. This inner strength helps us fight for what's important to us, so trusting in it only gives us more power.

When we become completely incongruent with our outer world, that is a sign that it's time for change. It means we are not living our truth, not living it out loud, and that can lead to some major misery down the line. Getting clear on what shifts we need to make to live our truth is essential. Then figuring out who are the people that matter in our lives and sharing it with them becomes key to start living it.

Isabelle and I wait two years to share our relationship with others to make sure it isn't "just a phase" - for us and as proof to our circle of family and friends that we are not temporary. In fact, we want to be so sure that when one of my closest friends comes out of the closet several months after Isabelle and I move in together, I still can't bring myself to share with him in that moment that I am in love with a woman.

Moving through all of the doubt, fear, and insecurities, when the time comes to ask myself if I believe in my connection with Isabelle; despite the fact that she is a woman, despite that I will have to face my family and friends with this reality, despite the lives it could flip upside down; my answer is a solid yes.

PART FOUR

Listen with your heart.

"Expose yourself to your deepest fear;
after that, fear has no power, and the
fear of freedom shrinks and vanishes.
You are free."

~ Jim Morrison

When we are ready to share our story with the people in our lives, we start the ball rolling with our parents. It is a big decision, but the right one to make. Moving forward in silence is no longer an option, so we grab our courage and determination with both hands and we jump into action.

I decide to tell my parents on the phone as we live an hour and a half apart, and now that I have mustered up the courage to tell them, I just want to get it out. Possibly disappointing my parents feels like I'm jumping off a cliff with no parachute. Up until now I have done everything in my life to gain their approval. Is this about to change?

So, on the phone is how it goes down. The important thing is that I share this monumental milestone in my life - that I am head over heels in love - and from that point on live my life more authentically.

I pick up the phone, my hands are trembling with fear, and my mouth is completely parched. I look at Isabelle one last time for encouragement, support, maybe a reason to do this later? But no! No, now is the time and I will not let my mind freak me out.

The phone rings and my mother answers, "Hello?"

"Hi Mom, how are you?" I say almost in a whisper.

"Good, how are you?" she replies.

"Good," and I immediately shift into gear to push myself to blurt out, "Mom, I have something to tell you." All right, there's no turning back now.

Hesitantly she says, "Okaaay..."

"Isabelle and I are together," I share quite bluntly, and then, complete silence.

After what is probably a brief pause, but to me feels like an hour, my mother says, "What do you mean?" as if I had just spoken in Chinese.

I reply, "We are together, as a couple."

This is followed by an even more awkward silence that feels to me like the length of an entire hockey game this time. The anguish and sheer terror that runs through me makes me want to drop the phone and run...but I stay...fighting the urge, hoping she isn't passed out on the floor.

I stay, but to be honest, it all becomes too much for me. My head is whirling, my heart is beating in my ears, and I feel like I'm the one about to pass out. The conversation does continue, and logically I know words are being shared and questions are being asked, but it's like I'm no longer the one there on the call, having this very important conversation with my mother. My nerves are so jacked up, I feel like I'm in an altered state and the result is loss of memory retention.

After we hang up, I sit in silence with Isabelle by my side, and I let all my thoughts and emotions whirl about me. Even though everything feels like a blur right now, I have enough clarity around the call to know that I was not instantly disowned, not at all. My parents may be in shock, but their love for me came through loud and clear. Already there are things I wish I could change about the crucial moment I just had with my mother. I wish I had gone into the call trusting more in the love that exists between my parents and me, and I wish I had the strength to sit down with them in person to live this experience. But the truth is I had heard so many horrific stories of other people sharing their similar experiences, that even though I was coming from a place of strength, I still needed to act in a way that fully supported me making this conversation happen at all. And I can live with that.

Once my head and body start to settle from my experience, my gaze shifts to Isabelle and the phone that lies in front of us. She takes in a deep breath and picks up the receiver.

Her experience with her mother happens in three distinct stages. Isabelle and her mother have a very open, very emotional connection in their communication. Crying around the dinner table at Isabelle's mother's house is not uncommon and oddly enough to me, not to be feared. They simply process feelings very quickly and in the moment. It's quite fascinating.

The first stage is Isabelle announcing to her mother on the phone that we are together. Being a dedicated Catholic, her mother's initial reaction upon hearing the news is, "Is it my fault?"

and their conversation rolls out from there, mostly with Isabelle answering more questions.

The immediate second stage to her mother's processing is throwing up. Now, this may sound a little dramatic, but you need to understand that Isabelle's mother lives everything to the fullest. The intensity with which she receives information and processes events in her life sometimes requires her to physically release when what she is processing is too much for her to absorb in the moment.

She is so stimulated by life that if she sees a bird land in her feeder outside, the whole world comes to a stop to enjoy the beauty that is this little bird. It is a true gift how simply she sees and processes every day life. Unfortunately, when the event is more controversial than a bird feeder, her reactions can be worrisome.

The third stage however, is one that saves our entire relationship with her moving forward. She decides to rush over to her own mother's house, her best friend, and it is Isabelle's grandmother who ends up helping her daughter through this difficult time. Isabelle's grandmother listens with the same familiar intensity and says one thing to provide guidance to her daughter and give her some perspective, "Let them live, they're not doing anything wrong."

As much as Isabelle's mother can live so intensely and hang on to her ideals, she also loves Isabelle unconditionally just as much - even when she is really struggling to understand her daughter's choices. After this initial day of sharing the news,

Isabelle waits three days before touching base with her mother again to give her time and space to process. When she finally does call, her mother says, "You haven't called me in three days! That's way too long!" And that's when Isabelle realizes they are going to be okay.

Several weeks pass by, and the moment arrives to tell my only sibling, my brother Steven. I drive five hours away to share this news with him in person. I do this because we are soon finishing our third year of university, and Isabelle and I have decided to move to Vancouver once we graduate after the summer semester. We are making sure to spend time with our parents before we move, however, my brother works summers at our uncle's fish hatchery, so this is my opportunity to make sure to see him in person before moving.

My brother and I have a rare and connected sibling relationship - one that started while he was in my mother's womb - and I will do anything to preserve it as I know way too many people who are estranged from their siblings.

When I was three years old my mother became pregnant. I remember being so happy that another child was coming into this world - especially this one. I would kiss my mother's belly every night before going to bed. One night I told her that she was going to give me a brother and his name would be Steven. I chose that name for two reasons. One, my favorite TV show character at the time was Steve Austin in an American series named *Six Million Dollar Man*. And two, like the bionic Steve Austin, I believed my brother would be a special hero.

Lo and behold, several months later, out came my brother and my parents felt they had no choice but to name him Steven. It's not every day a three-year-old demands a brother named Steven and he's delivered...literally.

So, to share my news with him, to be accepted and loved by him and have his support, is something I really need to feel before leaving for Vancouver. I drive the five hours to my aunt and uncle's fish hatchery and have a heart-to-heart face-to-face. We are sharing a room in the attic of their house, which is nice because it brings back many wonderful childhood memories of past Christmases and family summer holidays. We are sleeping in two twin beds, one opposite the other, and just before falling asleep I tell him about Isabelle. I am so nervous.

I mean this is the guy that literally saved me in high school when he was but a little elementary runt. The town I went to high school in had a very small English-speaking population, so the elementary and high school levels were merged in the same institution. Every year we were tested in our Physical Education class, and one of the tests was an Endurance Run. For the age I was at the time, this consisted of running 25 laps around the outdoor football field. Quite a huge undertaking for me, but I took the challenge on and started running.

I ran and ran and ran - lap after lap after lap with always too many left to the finish. I felt so out of breath my lungs burned, I stumbled and hallucinated, and even got sick to my stomach from lack of oxygen...I wanted to quit, I couldn't go on. I didn't know where I was going to find the energy, the strength, the "endurance" to finish this test. My teacher tried to give me words of encouragement, but I was so ready to throw in the towel - and that just wasn't me! I never quit on anything, especially a test!

As I slowly moved onward tripping over my feet, my eyes glazed over and visions of me sprawled out on the grass danced through my head; this tiny little face popped into my view out of nowhere. It was my brother, outside for the elementary recess, and he immediately got into stride with me, pulled me up and said, "We can finish this sis!"

At four years younger, and way more fit than I was or will ever be, his energy carried us both to that finish line. He stayed with me every step of the way, always encouraging, always keeping his belief in me up front and center. That endurance run by itself was such an unimportant event in the grand scheme of my life, but the love, support, and belief it created between my brother and I made it a pivotal moment I will never ever forget.

My heart pounds out of my chest as I speak to him up in that attic, because the thought of him rejecting our relationship and potentially walking out of my life, makes me ill. However, true to form once again, as soon as the words are out of my mouth about Isabelle, I hear him say through the darkness, "That's great! If she makes you happy, that's all that matters."

My heart does a back flip from happiness. His single response gives me the courage to tell the rest of the world. If he's on my side, I can handle any rejection that comes my way. He is a hero after all. My hero.

Later that summer after we graduate from university,

Isabelle and I prepare to leave where we've always called home to face the unknown. To end our existence as students and begin our lives as grown ups together.

One of the most life changing realizations I've ever had is that whatever I *think* is going to happen will always make a situation worse not better. Spending prescious time filled with anxiety, fear, doubt and setting expectations around something that hasn't even happened yet, is futile. When I finally share my truth with my family, I realize I am not trusting my love, my connection, and my relationship with them. Instead, I am *thinking* about everything that isn't there and not focusing on *feeling* what exists, and always has, between us.

The things I learn and explore from this experience and will share with you now are people who truly hold love in their hearts for us will work through challenges in time, people come and go in a lifetime and there is always a reason, and people may not want to be loved in the same manner as we desire to be loved. Remain open to everyone in our lives despite the fear and learn to recognize that love may show up differently for some than for others – but it's still love.

1.People who truly hold love in their heart for us will work it out.

By loving the people who matter to us, enough to let them go in intense situations that require a processing of feelings, we hold space for them to return to us. It may take a month, like it may take a few years, like it may take no time at all. If the people we care about truly hold love in their heart for us and are in a place to learn and grow from the experience, they will return. Our paths may separate, but they will find each other again. Staying true to ourselves is key and trusting the people who matter are still meant to be in our lives. Speaking our truth is a commitment we all need to make to ourselves. A commitment to our happiness and to our level of fulfillment.

When communicating our truth, always share from the heart. Developing a strong ability for heart-driven communication, always connecting to what feels right within ourselves, will encourage people to listen with the same intention of love - and that is our best chance to being understood and seen. Genuine, authentic communication speaks volumes, and although nerves and fear may push us to rush through what we need to share, being patient and staying present, allows our words to be absorbed and reflected upon.

Regardless of how and when we deliver our truth, time is a gift. Granting our loved ones time to process is a sign of respect and importance, because even if it takes a long time, the bond of love is more eternal than hate ever will be. My mother still wishes I had told my father and her about Isabelle and me in person, and I completely understand her perspective on the importance of seeing them to share this major news, but the reality is I just couldn't do it at the time. It took every ounce of me to share my relationship with her over the phone, let alone look into their eyes as I did it. In the end, the important thing is I then gave my parents time to digest and process this information to come to their own decisions about it without any further pressure from me. I finally placed all my trust in their love for me and then simply let go.

It needs to be said that even as a full grown, very well established, and balanced adult, I still somehow seek my parents' approval in ways. At the age of 36 I get my first tattoo. And even at that age, I show up to my parents' home and start nervously weaseling my way into a conversation, saying I have something to share with them as I twist my fingers together and feel my temperature start to rise.

Come. On.

My father is a man that loves to guess things, especially birthday and Christmas presents. He is one of those that will shake, smell, and weigh a gift prior to opening it to see if he can guess its contents. The frustrating part is most of the time he ends up being right! Still to my surprise my Dad jokingly says to my nervous display, "What? Did you get a tattoo?"

I look at him in disbelief and shockingly say, "Yes!"

Immediately both my parents ask to see the said tattoo and of course I show them. My mother, having sensed my discomfort in announcing this news says, "You're a grown woman Maggie, what does it matter if we approve of you getting a tattoo or not?"

And she's right, yet still somewhere deep down I need

to know if they support my decisions and, in this case, action. I guess for me, because my parents are the people who instilled my values and largely shaped me into the woman I am today, I still see them as a very important guiding light in my life. Since taking two years to tell them about my relationship with Isabelle, I have also become very sensitive to sharing big events in my life in a timelier fashion. My first tattoo at the age of 36 is a big event for me and sharing it feels right.

If we show the people in our lives that we care deeply for them by sharing our truth with them and not requiring immediate responses, we are telling them we trust them with our heart and showing them some compassion for what they are going through as well. If they don't return to our lives, then they are most likely not ready to receive what the experience is teaching them. And that's okay too. It is an honor to witness anyone's truth. It is the most authentic human experience.

2. Be open to who matters. People come and go in a lifetime, and there is always a reason.

If something is truly right for us, know that deep down approval from others is not essential for our happiness - it is a blessing. Approval is about the people with whom we share our truth, not about us living our own truth. It is about their capacity to love and not judge. If they step to the plate and show up, then they are meant to continue participating in our lives. If they don't show up, it's probably time for them to move on anyway.

My parents love me through everything, including learning about my relationship with Isabelle. Of course, they need time to process and wrap their heads around what I am living, but they never stop loving me through it all and I never feel judged. I do ask my mother to help me fill in the blanks about our conversation on the phone that day when I finally shared what I had been keeping in for so long. She reveals that the silence after my initial declaration was because she had a lump in her throat and couldn't speak. Fair enough, it was quite the bomb to drop. She also shares she remembers me speaking with anger. She says I told her she could take care of sharing the news with the rest of the family. This really surprises me as I don't recall that at all, but I very well could have said that as a protection mechanism in a panic to check out and avoid further conflict. That's me – peacemaker to the core.

What I am most grateful for is that my parents chose to continue to love me through the circumstances. That was a true gift. Feeling the support of our own love and not judging ourselves is even more crucial. Being sure about our choices, that they are right for us is important. If we make the choice out of love for ourselves and go with our heart, we can face whatever gets put in our path. We may lose people, and if they don't come back in our lives it's because their own journey doesn't allow them to forgive or put their love for us first at this point and time.

Also know that it can be surprising who shows up in our lives when we keep our heart open and allow new connections to form. It is important to share our happiness with the people that

Approval is about
the people with whom
we share our truth,
not about us living
our own truth.

do continue or start to participate in our lives, because the new connections will replace the old. That is guaranteed. When we create space in our lives, whether chosen or not, the Universe sees that we have room to receive and complies. Support is out there, especially if our current support system disintegrates. The more we can connect with people, the more opportunities we create to continue building our network of friends and supporters. No matter where we are in our lives, there are people out there who see us for who we are at the core. It's simply a question of do we already know them, or have we just not met them yet?

The beautiful thing about sharing our truth is that it creates an imaginary playing field that existing relationships either need to show up for or walk away from, and new ones get to decide if they want to participate. Either way connecting to our heart raises the standards in our lives, for ourselves and for the people we share our lives with moving forward.

3. People may not want to be loved in the same manner as we desire to be loved.

Just like everyone has fingerprints, but they are different from person to person; everyone has the capacity to love, but the way in which they like to receive love can be different from person to person. One thing remains the same however, and that is all the ways to love come from the heart.

There are five different love languages according to Dr. Gary Chapman, author of *The Five Love Languages: How to Express Heartfelt Commitment to Your Mate.*

1. Words of Affirmation
2. Acts of Service
3. Receiving Gifts
4. Quality Time
5. Physical Touch

Generally, the type of love we give is the type of love we like to receive. So, as a loving partner, or even as a friend or family member, it is our duty to figure out which types of love our people cherish, and to give it to them in that way. Even if it is completely different from what we give naturally or the kind of love expression we like to experience. The point is our love shows through when we make the effort to love out of deep care and respect for the person receiving.

Once we figure out how someone likes to be loved, it is just as important to acknowledge the love we receive from them. Saying thank you to the efforts and the hearts of the people who love us is recognizing them at a spiritual level. It is seeing them for the beings that they are and rejoicing in the love that unites us all.

We are blessed with life and being grateful for the love that does show up in our lives is so important. Gratitude keeps us grounded and links us to a higher power. It allows us to see the good in our daily lives. Love shows up in big and small ways, and to recognize all its forms as a gift, keeps us present. Love is all-seeing and can change people - because it empowers us to shift.

PART FIVE

Let love lead.

"No one is born hating another
person because of the color of his skin,
or his background, or his religion.
People must learn to hate, and if they can
learn to hate, they can be taught to love,
for love comes more naturally to the
human heart than its opposite."

~ Nelson Mandela

U pon finishing university in the summer of '94 Isabelle and I move to Vancouver. We each graduate from Concordia with a BFA Specialization in Design for the Theatre. We want to use our new skills in the film industry, and the film industry action is happening out in Western Canada. So, we sell everything we own, rent a car, and drive across Canada to Vancouver to begin our life outside of school.

We arrive in Vancouver, eventually find an apartment, and buy what we need with the money we made from our furniture sale in Montreal. We apply for membership in the film industry union and jump through all their hoops to be able to work on a set. We finally make it onto the call list and are told to wait until they have an opportunity. Great! Good things are happening, and we are excited to wait for the phone to ring.

It doesn't take us long to learn that in 1994, the union uses an alphabetical system to call members when an opening comes up for a TV show or movie. My last name starts with an "R" and Isabelle's with a "T", so we are shit out of luck.

In the meantime, we make the most of our new life in Vancouver and settle into living out in the open with our friends and everyone in our families. Everyone except my Italian grandparents, my father's parents. I feel horrible about it, but they are very traditional and Catholic, and the Romano family decides it is for the best to keep them in the dark. My grandparents are getting on in years and wrapping their heads around the whole concept of a same-sex relationship in their own family feels like it might be too much for them to handle at this stage. I find it unfortunate that my loving bliss is considered a "concept", but you choose your battles, right? And this is one I can let go of in the spirit of keeping my grandparents surrounded by love and in a healthy state of mind.

My grandparents, being the good Italian people that they are, make it their mission to ask me at every visit, "Do you have a boyfriend?" with a nice undertone of "Italian of course!" They see me as prime marriage material and I should actually be quite grateful that they haven't already picked out and promised me to a nice Italian boy.

It tears me up to say "No, I don't have a boyfriend," to my little munchkin nonno and nonna, and I convince myself that technically I'm not lying. Isabelle is indeed a woman, and therefore very much my *girl*friend. And very much French. Yikes.

One day, my grandfather asks his daughter, my aunt, about Isabelle and me. He's no dummy. He sees how we are around each other when we visit even if we are careful - along with my consistent negative response to the boyfriend question - and he's putting two and two together. My aunt is very hesitant to divulge to the patriarch of our family the answer to his question, but she cannot tell a lie to her father. So, with courage in hand my aunt tells him about us.

Apparently, you could hear a pin drop when my aunt first lets him in on the truth about my relationship with Isabelle... until he magically breaks the silence with, "I knew it! We had that kind of business in my day too you know!" He then turns to my grandmother, "Told you so!"

We. Are. Dumbfounded. Thrilled. And basically, blown away all at the same time. For us to have seriously misjudged him is so unfair, and that is not lost on me. We are ecstatically surprised at this news, and what's better is he loves Isabelle even more after that. They get along like two unfiltered peas in a pod. They make the whole family laugh and that is beautiful.

About a year later, once again we face uncertainty in outing our relationship. Isabelle starts a new job as a graphic designer and her new boss shares with her early in the working relationship that she really doesn't agree with nor understand same-sex relationships. Isabelle is a little relieved that she has not yet shared our relationship status at work because as it turns out, that would have been a very interesting welcome. It's crazy, by this point we have been together four years, our family and friends know about us and support us, and we are still dealing with issues of acceptance and judgment. Yet somehow, we both know that we will face this issue to some degree for the rest of our days together.

Several months go by. Isabelle and I, along with her boss and her boss' boyfriend, hang out as friends from time to time and get to know each other better. There's a great rapport between us because we are all French Canadians living in Vancouver, and that gives us much to talk about. Plus, we have fun together. Laughter is a constant companion, despite the occasional uneasiness Isabelle and I experience when having to bite our tongues to not divulge our relationship.

One day at work, Isabelle's boss is generalizing about what she believes "gay people" to be, and she has deducted all of this based on what makes it through to the media. Public indecency scandals, the spread of AIDS, and let's face it - pride parades don't give same-sex couples the image of committed, conservative people.

Today, Isabelle has about enough of this talk and cuts her boss off in her rant. "You know, not ALL gay people are like that," she blurts out.

"Really? How do you know?" says her boss.

Isabelle hesitates then lets out what she's been dying to say for months, "I know because Margarita and I have been happily together for over four years!"

The words wrap the tiny frame of Isabelle's boss in surprise and immediately render her speechless. You can see the images of the loving friendship that has blossomed between the four of us whiz through her mind as she gives Isabelle's declaration serious thought. She stands there in disbelief, witnessing her perception of the "gay world" shatter around her and fall to the floor.

About six years later, Isabelle and I hold a 10-year commitment ceremony at our friends' horse ranch in the Cariboo in British Columbia, a five-hour drive from Vancouver. We invite an intimate group of family and close friends as our witnesses, including Isabelle's now ex-boss and her young six-year-old daughter.

To our heartfelt surprise, she stands up during the ceremony holding her daughter's hand and shares, "I wish for my daughter to experience a love as beautiful as yours. Congratulations!"

This moment touches our hearts in such a profound way, because we know the journey she has been on to get to this place of peace, and we appreciate the deep transformation she has undergone. It gives us faith to continue to live our love courageously.

This ceremony represents a special right of passage for Isabelle and me on so many levels. Mostly because it unites for the first time our two worlds. Our blood family from the east of Canada with our family of friends from the west of Canada. When Isabelle and I moved to Vancouver we surrounded ourselves over the years with a truly outstanding group of people that we consider family. Having these two important parts of our lives mingle and merge at our commitment ceremony is a blessing and a gift.

After the ceremony we all sit down to a very impressive

ranch-style dinner. There are lit candles in the chandeliers that are tastefully decorated with fresh flowers, everyone is smiling and laughing, and the air is filled with love and magic. I sit back for a moment and take it all in. I couldn't have dreamed of a better outcome. I am grateful beyond words for the love that surrounds me every day. And just when I think the moment can't get any better, my father puts his arm around me and tops it all by saying, "I get it now."

I think up until that point he had always wondered why Isabelle and I had trekked all the way across Canada to build our lives. The four simple words he says to me that evening tell me he now understands what Vancouver holds for us. It holds acceptance, happiness, love...and possibility. It moves me so much to hear those words come from my father. I didn't realize I needed to hear him say that, until he said it.

Later that night the Northern Lights come out to play and magically shower us with a wonderful sense of fulfillment. As we gaze at the shining stars, we feel the bigness of the Universe as well as the love of the people no longer with us. It surrounds us with peace and in that moment, we know everything is as it should be.

have shared the pivotal moments with my grandparents and Isabelle's boss to demonstrate two things. One, never underestimate people and their capacity to love. And two, time can shift and change a person if they love you unconditionally. The lessons I learn from this time in my life with a heart full of gratitude are that love is a beautiful language that not only crosses boundaries but removes them completely, keeping an open heart holds endless possibilities, and love is a two-way street that allows us to give and take.

1. The essence of love is a language that crosses time, culture, age, religion, and gender.

Love is universal. It is an unbiased state of being that everyone can attain and connect with because it is felt within and shared with others. Have you ever shared a moment of perfectly clear communication with someone without even speaking the same language? That is love speaking - that universal connection to all things.

I remember at our 10-year commitment ceremony, I watched a conversation happen between one of my dearest friends and Isabelle's mother. My friend spoke English and Isabelle's mother spoke French. One would ask a question in one language and the other would answer in the other language. The whole scene was quite beautiful, as I could understand both sides, and could feel they were really connecting on a whole other level. The heart level. It wasn't about the actual words coming out of their mouths, it was about what each was expressing non-verbally. That expression, that wavelength is love. They hugged each other in a special moment at the end of the conversation and both looked elated from the exchange.

The earlier we learn to live from a place of love, the more open we become to fully experience life. Love unfolds our experiences, and what this world has to offer, in a whole new light. Love connects us to a higher power, something much larger than ourselves, and this connection brings enormous amounts of joy and sensitivity. This sensitivity acts like a radar, allowing us to notice the little things that bring fulfillment. The things we can easily gloss over when stuck in our daily routines and numb from the busy-ness of life.

I meet a young and beautiful woman from New York while writing the first draft of this book in Bali. She's in Bali on a similar journey, and on an overnight excursion to an island close by, she experiences the international language of love with a little Indonesian boy on the beach and shares it with me.

"Love knows no language or barriers," she says. "After watching me sketch the symbols for 'wishes intentions prayers' in the sand and then watching the ocean wash it away - this little boy comes over to trace my heart and cross once again in the sand. We speak no words only hearts and smiles." Children instinctively know how to speak love. It is what we learn and experience as we grow up that conditions us to slowly lose this intuition.

Never underestimate someone's connection to love. In writing this book, I can't help but realize how open to love both

Love is universal.
It is an unbiased
state of being that
everyone can attain
and connect with
because it is felt
within and shared
with others.

Isabelle's grandmother and my grandparents were at a time in our lives when love was under scrutiny. Isabelle's grandmother helped her daughter to accept us through love, and my grandfather was nowhere near surprised to find out that his granddaughter was in love with a woman. In fact, he was very accepting of and loving to me.

We have met and heard of people much younger than our grandparents, people brought up in a much more inclusive and accepting time, still treating others who do not look or act like themselves with disrespect and dislike. And, the very people we assumed would be most close-minded ended up being accepting and without judgment; which allows me to believe that anyone can choose to reconnect with the universal love we instinctively tune into as children. At any age, we can choose to return to that state of being that resides in us all, and that to me is hope. Hope that we are never too far away from unconditional love, even when it is hardest to feel it. All we need to do is decide to open our heart.

2. Keep our heart open - anything can happen.

A closed heart does not allow for happiness. In fact, a closed heart blocks not only the joy from getting out, but also the joy from being let in. Yes, opening our heart makes us vulnerable and susceptible to being hurt, and as we all know being hurt is not fun. However, opening our heart also increases our level of happiness and sense of fulfillment. And the great thing is, the more we keep our heart open to experiencing love and all the good it brings, the less time we spend in anguish and sorrow. It doesn't mean we'll never feel hurt again, but it does mean that the time we do spend in sorrow can become less and less as we increase our desire and drive to return to love and an open heart.

The one thing for sure in this world is nothing is permanent. Anything can change, and that includes our ideals and beliefs. We can never be certain how someone will react when love, values, and trust are tested. We may think we know with family members, partners, and close friends, but we really don't. Why? Because love changes everything, especially unconditional love. Things that were easily rejected in the past, may be accepted in the future. If we allow love to grow within us, the world and how we participate in it, becomes a whole new playground.

Believe it or not, I have witnessed a beautiful example of just how much good unconditional love can do, within a herd of horses. The beautiful horses that are now in my life. When Kahlua, a 21-year-old gelding joined my existing herd of two, he was labeled "The horse you do not put with other horses". There was something about Kahlua though, that I recognized from the first moment I saw his photo. He was special and most of all, wanted to change. When I met him in person I felt he was asking me to help him drop the label. And so, my herd and I welcomed him with open arms, love, support and trust.

I then proceeded to watch my 13-year-old gelding Cache, show Kahlua what it means to be a part of a herd. Cache who was always a dominant horse, stood patiently by Kahlua in quiet confidence as Kahlua tested Cache in every way possible. He would run at him, bite him, kick him, and Cache would not fight back. He would hold a loving space and walk away from Kahlua every time, giving Kahlua whatever he was so forcefully asking for – whether it was food, the shelter, or standing by our mare Powder. He was showing Kahlua that there was another way to be, within a herd and with people.

Over a short period of time, Kahlua quickly developed a sensitivity to the herd dynamics at play. The consistency in love and acceptance that Cache, Powder, and I showed Kahlua every day began to teach him a new way of being. Cache slowly shifted from allowing Kahlua space to hold tantrums, to starting to teach him what is acceptable behavior and what is not. Powder and I followed Cache's lead. Because we all gave him space initially, Kahlua trusted us enough to learn from us...and today he is very much a horse living amongst a herd. In fact, he is an integral part of the herd, with his own role and job. He is still a very spicy horse with a colorful character, and we love that about him, however he is learning to trust which creates the desire to love the ones around him too.

Impressing ourselves with how much we are capable of loving, is one of the biggest gifts we could ever give ourselves because we reap the rewards 100-fold. The more we love and give, the more we receive and grow. The more we care about the world, the more the world reveals and shares its beauty with us.

3. Support the people who love you – love is a two-way street.

Be the first to care for, check-in on, give to and forgive the people who matter. We are all human, and humans always have and always will make mistakes, bad judgment calls, and stick our foot where it doesn't belong. This is human nature. Take the first step forward anyway, and give that long-lost friend a call, or bring a grumpy sick sibling some chicken noodle soup. Take your mother out to lunch even though she is constantly meddling in your life. Don't let petty disagreements waste time that could be spent in love. Whenever the feeling grabs you, hug the person you are with - hugs benefit both the giver and the receiver. It's not enough to tell people we love them - show them as well. Love is an energy that vibrates between two beings and hugging raises that vibration.

According to Lindsay Holmes, an associate editor for *The Huffington Post*, "The simple act of a hug isn't just felt on our arms. When we embrace someone, oxytocin (also known as 'the cuddle hormone') is released, making us feel all warm and fuzzy inside. The chemical has also been linked to social bonding."

Further studies have shown that hugs can also help our physical health, and significantly reduce worry of mortality. Not to mention they are just so damn fun to experience!

I remember one day I reached out to a friend that I was having a rough time and feeling very emotional and alone. Without me knowing, she left work, hopped right into her car, and drove all the way to my house simply to give me chocolate and a very long heartfelt hug. That hug filled the empty part of me with such goodness, it turned my day around and most of all, gave me hope.

Another way to support the people we love is to focus on *how* we choose to do something rather than *what* we actually do. Intention behind action goes a long way. A big part of what makes a good massage is not just technique, but the energy and intention the massage therapist puts into the technique. If a massage therapist focuses on their shitty day during a massage, we will feel that even though what they are doing is technically correct.

Same with our tone. If we can put love into every word that we communicate and every action we perform, not only will we feel terrific for giving from the heart, but the person receiving will positively shift because of that love.

Love lives through the good and the bad. When a loved one passes, and we look back, it's not the mistakes that person made that we tend to hang on to, but more the love that was shared. So, imagine how much this world could positively shift if we all focus on the love we share with people while everyone is still alive? How much better would life be?

I realize some things are harder to forgive and move on from than others, and these situations need to be felt and processed – however, if we can find the strength to make letting go a part of our process, we only benefit from loving ourselves enough to move forward - whether that person remains in our lives or not.

PART SIX

Be patient.

"Life will give you whatever experience is most helpful for the evolution of your consciousness."

~ Eckhart Tolle

Before Isabelle gets the job as a graphic designer, there is a short stint for us both as security guards. Isabelle, standing outside directing traffic for 12 hours in the rain, chaffing her neck raw from constantly looking one side to the other in a polyester uniform - does not make for a happy woman. Luckily, I am right by her side and a tad more patient. I even get into the spirit of it all and without entirely thinking it through, shave my head - you know, to look tough! I learn quite quickly however the true art of patience as I begin to hear the endless hollers of "sir" or "pal" whenever my back is turned to someone. Luckily my...ummm...feminine assets correct that behavior pretty much effortlessly every time I turn around.

One ridiculously cold night, Isabelle and I are both working in the cruise ship terminal in Vancouver, literally making sure no one climbs the Christmas trees that are on display for the seasonal show. We have the night shift, so let's just say there is no one in sight and the night is ticking beyond slow. We each take a section of the terminal and make our rounds of the trees, ensuring no ornament has decided to go rogue from boredom.

It's eerily quiet and bone chillingly cold. We are doing everything not to fall asleep, but our bodies insist on enticing us to shut down and hibernate. Suddenly, over the loud speaker an authoritative voice clearly demands, "Tango 8, this is OPS Control, please come to the office."

Isabelle's call sign that evening is Tango 8. We meet in the middle of the terminal and Isabelle says, "I have to go, it's all yours."

I jokingly tell her I'm pretty sure I can handle it but will call for back-up if I need it. I may not be a spy, but I think I have what it takes to diffuse a situation between an ornament and a Christmas tree. So, with a wink in my direction, she goes upstairs to respond to the call from Operations Control Center - the eyes of the building.

Isabelle never returns that night. I worry something bad has happened, but I can't leave my post, and this is pre-everyone-has-a-cell-phone era, therefore I need to wait until my shift is over to hopefully see her at home? So, I finish the night and leave as soon as the clock hits the hour - I am so ready for bed I'm exhausted, but my worry walks me all the way to our apartment while the city is buzzing with everyone just starting their day.

I finally get home, and I do not expect what awaits me when I walk through the door. Isabelle is vibrating with a mixture of rage and excitement...a very unlikely combination.

I am still taking my shoes off when Isabelle explodes

with, "When I got to OPS Control, they immediately accused me of letting two children climb up a fuckin' Christmas tree. Can you believe it??? I said to them, 'Are you crazy? Take a closer look at your little TVs buddy, there's no one in sight!' You should see the amount of security monitors they have up there. They can see every corner of the cruise ship terminal."

I am now leaning against the front door of our small, one-bedroom apartment in disbelief. Children? There were no children there in the middle of the damn night! I know, I was there! There were barely even any adults...children? As I stare at Isabelle, the only sound that escapes my lips is, "What???"

"They insisted that I was not doing my job, and no one tells me that. No one. I'm disgusted with them!" Isabelle says in all her French fierceness.

I can feel the hurt behind Isabelle's words at this point... and I get it. Isabelle excels at many things, and her work ethic is above and beyond any of them. It is one of the many things I love about her, and so I understand her feelings of betrayal, especially when we both know there had been no one other than her and me in that terminal for several hours.

She continues, "After 15 minutes of accusations, which quite frankly demonstrated an enormous amount of patience on my part, I unhooked my two-way radio from my pants and slammed it on the desk saying, 'Consider this my fuckin' resignation!' and I stormed out."

With my eyes bulging from my head I respond, "Ya know, for a girl who just picked up the English language, you certainly have mastered the art of swearing," and I giggle. This made her pause with a smile, and then jump right back into her recount of the night.

"I was so mad Maggie, I ripped off every piece of my uniform and left a trail down the hallway to the locker room. Just before I went in, our British Boss popped out of nowhere and stopped me in my tracks. He had the nerve to say to me, 'Isabelle, don't worry about what OPS Control says, we'll smooth it out. You're on shift for the next seven days. Please!'"

At this I needed to laugh. The image of our poor security manager having to deal with the sudden loss of one of his best guards was too much. Especially when this guard was Isabelle in a rage. I did feel for him though, I know he meant what he said.

In true form Isabelle goes on, "I kid you not, standing there in front of him in my tank top and underwear I smiled and told him, 'I'm sorry, but there is no way in hell I'm staying here to be mistreated in that manner.'"

"And then do you know what he said to me?" she says eyes bulging. "He said, 'You can't do this!'"

Giving me the evil eye meant for our manager, she continues, "I can't do this?!? Oh yeah? Watch me! I said to him and then went into the locker room with the door swinging behind me. I got dressed, headed across the street to the unemployment office and immediately applied for a job as a graphic designer! A trade I actually have a degree in and a position that pays almost three times what I'm making as a security guard!!!"

And there it is, I now understand the underlying

excitement I first sensed in her rage. Before I met Isabelle, she had taken some pre-university courses to get her degree in Graphic Design. A three-year program she of course managed to accomplish in two years. See? Work ethic.

I jump into her arms at this point and give her a massive hug saying, "Honey, you're incredible! Truly! I am so proud of you. You deserve to get this job, and in a way, I am grateful to this horrible night because it has sent you to where you deserve to be. Creating, and not directing traffic."

Isabelle ends up getting this position upon being interviewed. Her bravery, courage, and belief in herself are remarkable. As uncomfortable as it is to think about it, I know I have met her to grow in these areas, to step out from the shadows and stand up for who I am. I love that I get to journey with this wonderful person. That's my girl. Yes.

Needless to say but I will, Isabelle is a little bit of an impatient person. Leaving the security job and getting the graphic design job puts her in her place of power and she is not tolerating a thing. So, when the film union that we joined ages ago finally calls us for a job that we must show up for in 10 minutes or they take us off the list - and we live an hour away - Isabelle easily and generously gives them a piece of her mind and slams down the phone. We never hear from them again. Ever.

Because of this, after a short time we end up starting our first graphic design business together part-time, and without a second thought I put my desire to be in the theatre and film industry aside. Isabelle is so driven and passionate about life that

I willingly choose to follow her anywhere - and it isn't until many years later that I realize just how big this is, choosing someone else's path over my own.

Within the first year of the business, Isabelle leaves her graphic designer position to work for our company full-time. I leave the shift work of my security job to work full-time in a credit department for a telecommunications company to bring in some consistent money in the meantime. Yes, I get paid to take severe verbal abuse from people who cannot pay their bills all so that we can afford basic living costs while we start up our graphic design studio. Despite the abuse, this job does have a better salary and way better hours than my prestigious security guard position ever did. It allows me to manage our new business at nights and on weekends, and this is perfect for now.

We are thrilled to be working together. In school, we had such a similar work ethic, and we complement each other so well in life, that we just know we'll be great business partners.

And we are, great business partners. So much so that the business booms very quickly and within the second year I quit my job and we officially become full-time business partners in 1996. We are winning business and creative awards and working with some very big corporations. The more we grow, the more Isabelle pours herself into her work and time flies by.

As her business partner, I adore her dedication to making our company successful. As her life partner, I feel like we are losing ourselves and growing apart. I'm not very good at communicating my feelings on the spot and tend to suppress whatever is bothering me for fear of conflict. So, instead of addressing what's no longer working for me as the feelings arise, I leave Isabelle in the dark about what my heart is experiencing.

This goes on for a while, Isabelle continues to focus on her work and I grow lonelier and lonelier, until one very special day when I decide to speak up and share with Isabelle what's on my mind. Unfortunately, I have waited so long to talk to her that what simply should have been about sharing my feelings, comes out more like an ultimatum.

"I can't do this anymore Isabelle, you have to choose - me or your work," I say with complete seriousness and a great sense of relief at finally having said something. Honestly at this point, a big part of me really thinks Isabelle will choose her work and simply turn around and leave - much like she did at the cruise ship terminal that day she ditched all her clothes. It is for this very reason I take so long to voice my discontent in the first place. I need to be ready for whatever shows up.

What she says next surprises the hell out of me. She immediately says, "Holy Shit!" and in her next breath, "Ok, we are shutting down the business this week and doing what it takes to get us back on track."

We then spend every day of that week sitting on a sandy beach talking, crying, laughing, crying, talking, and working it out until we finally reach the point of make-up sex. I am wholeheartedly impressed with Isabelle's devotion to our relationship, still am to this day. A big lesson in speaking up occurs for me in this moment. Isabelle has me realize that my feelings and what I have to say are valued, even more than her inspiring work, and that gives me wings. I also realize that she deserves to know about my feelings way before I reach the point of ultimatum. We had no chance to course correct in this case. It was all or nothing - we went from a fully functioning business to none, to deal with what was happening.

We move forward after that week - older, wiser, and connected as a couple like never before. We create boundaries around personal and work time, take time to travel as a couple and with family and friends, and innovate with our business and team to produce work we are all proud to share.

Until six years later, when the sudden death of a very dear friend prompts us to really understand how short life is and that it's up to us to make the most of our time here. His death at the young age of 47 makes us think hard about what we each want in the next phase of our lives. Isabelle and I have been trying to integrate more strategic brand work with our clients and prospects at this point, as that is where we now want to play. However, we are continuously pegged as the ladies who create great marketing material, and they turn to other strategists for the more internal work we are wanting to help them develop. It feels like we are dragging our existing business somewhere it doesn't want to go, and this makes our successful graphic design firm no longer fun for us - and life's too short to not have fun. So, we decide to sell our creative business and travel the world for a year.

We start the year off easy in an all-inclusive in Mexico. The first item on our agenda of our year off is to sleep, veg, tan, eat, and repeat. And we do this quite successfully, with only a little interlude of zip-lining and rappelling to satisfy our sense of adventure.

From there we go to Bali with Isabelle's parents to explore and expand our horizons in a different culture, a culture we have never experienced before. We love the Balinese and truly absorb and enjoy the time and intention they put into everything. It helps us slow down our mind, body, and spirit to create a deeper sense of awareness.

After that we pack one bag, get in our Mini Cooper, and begin a three-month road trip across the United States and Canada. Things are going wonderfully well as we are relaxing, enjoying each other's company, and laughing again - we are having fun. So much so, that on a few days of down time on our road trip - as we must deal with a flat tire from exploring a sunflower field in the Prairies and ending up stuck in clay - we make the spontaneous decision to join two of our dearest friends and travel Vietnam and Cambodia together once we return to Vancouver. We are so excited to meet up with them as they have been traveling as well for a couple of months now, and we cannot wait to see them.

About a week later, we are back in Vancouver and at the airport leaving for Hong Kong. Upon arrival at the airport in Danang, Vietnam, our friends are waiting to greet us with a sign that says, "Canadian Babes Traveling". Woohoo! That's us all right and we're ready to continue our adventure.

And that it is, an adventure. We see, taste, hear, and smell so many things, I don't even know where to begin telling you about them all and we are soaking up every experience. By this time Isabelle and I have been together for 15 years. In fact, we celebrate our anniversary on this very trip! Our friends that we are traveling with have been together for about a year and are still very much in the honeymoon phase. Little do we know that witnessing their young love will really have us "look" at each other and question after all these years, do we still want the same things out of life?

Three days stuck in one hotel room in one tiny village on the coast of Vietnam due to a storm allows us to find out. The Universe really does work in mysterious ways, doesn't it? These three days for Isabelle and me, blend magically into feeling like one extremely long day. One that begins with a lot of soul-searching, crying, and pretty much leaving each other, to coming out the other side and finding common ground again. This time there are no ultimatums. This time there's authentic communication and a multitude of conversations. As many as it takes to speak our truth and feel like we are truly being heard. The result is a strong desire that is created between her and I to continue to work things out and move forward together.

Relationships take work, and lots of it. And it doesn't matter if it's a relationship with your lover, your mother, or your boss — they all take work. They take work because we are human beings with emotions, and we are constantly evolving, growing, and changing.

The main realizations I want to introduce in this part of the book are these. Love is not always roses and cupids, don't fear the bad as it makes us stronger and moves us forward, and always remember to love is to serve – but not at the expense of our own selves. These realizations are pivotal to our personal growth, as well as the growth of our relationships.

1. Love is not always roses and cupids...in fact love that lasts a lifetime never is.

To love means loving the unlovable just as much. Love encompasses all, the good, the bad, and the ugly. If it doesn't, then it's not really love. When someone close to our heart tests our love, the authenticity of that love is what is put to the test. This doesn't mean we need to accept bad behavior and live with it, but it does mean our ability to love ourselves and to forgive another is challenged.

In their very early years, Isabelle and her younger brother were inseparable. They did everything together, even had their own secret language! They were the best of friends and could always count on each other to have the finest laughing fits ever.

When Isabelle turned 14 her parents decided to get a divorce, and although Isabelle was satisfied that this event was going to return peace to the household – her very sensitive brother did not feel the same way. He took the divorce hard and it showed through a series of behavioral shifts. The first few years after the divorce coincided with her brother falling into the wrong crowd at the wrong time, and theft became a coping mechanism. As time went on and he continued to suppress his many feelings, he added substance abuse to his roster. Things kept progressing from bad to worse.

Throughout the years, Isabelle extended many lines of help to her younger brother – from a place to stay and food to eat, to lending him money and giving him clothes and furniture. Although her heart was in the right place, this kind of love she was bestowing upon him only enabled his destructive behavior and often his actions ended up hurting Isabelle deeply. Before long, trust shattered between the two siblings and it tore Isabelle apart to come to the realization that the relationship she used to cherish with her brother, no longer existed.

Isabelle's devastation led her to discover a different way of loving her brother. A way that stemmed from loving herself first and forgiving him in the process. By placing her needs first, she created the boundaries she needed with her brother to no longer enable him. She chose to not participate in the drama of his life and instead, chooses to enjoy him for who he is at the core when she is with him. She now lets her love connect to his spirit, the one that makes her laugh and enjoy his company and leaves his addiction to the experts. She has forgiven her brother for the many ways he hurt her, and the trust they used to share may or may not return. However, Isabelle has found a way to embrace a love for her brother that has brought her peace, more than anger and resentment ever could.

As I mentioned in the beginning, I was raised on respect, respect is huge for me. What it teaches me is that people deserve our very best, regardless of whether they do the same. We cannot control others, but we are responsible for our own actions. So, might as well use those actions wisely.

Love in all its forms is a gift that teaches us about ourselves. Whether we need to be more open, trust, or forgive more - love is the foundation that allows us to explore what we need without fear. The paradox however, is that most people carry fear around love because of the past. If we can find the strength to move beyond past hurt or rejection, love can allow us to heal and reach new personal horizons.

2. Don't fear the bad as it makes us stronger and moves us forward.

Embracing fear goes against human nature. Period. No matter how much we can claim to look fear in the face, our bodies still react in some way to the experience. Whether it feels like our stomachs are flipping upside down, we are shaking from head to toe, or we literally turn around and run away - fear creates a physical reaction within us because we are born with an instinct to protect ourselves physically and mentally.

What's important is to acknowledge the fear within us and then move past it. One way I have found to successfully achieve this is to focus on what I know in my heart I'm meant to do - regardless of the odds. Hearts do not lie, minds will to protect us. If we can find the strength to listen to what our heart is telling us in these moments of fear and act upon it, even if it goes against what everyone else believes, then we will in some way finally be looking fear in the face. We are dealing with the fear, and therefore eliminating that fear from our lives.

John Ashley-Pryce had a good marriage. He and his wife shared a relationship based on a solid foundation of friendship and love. Despite this, seven years into their marriage John found himself becoming increasingly more interested in a close friend of the couple. This close friend is named Doug.

John and Doug were symbiotic in many ways and they soon found themselves doing things together more and more on their own, until the day came that it truly sunk in - they realized they were falling in love. This realization shook John's soul. He had such respect and love for his wife yet knew his feelings for Doug were undeniable and that Doug was what his heart wanted. John needed to do some serious soul searching to have any chance of revealing his truth. So, one day he decided to climb Mt. Seymour in Vancouver on his own to get some clarity. He tried to determine what he'd done, how he got there, and what his choices were moving forward. The more he processed, the more he thought, how was he going to leave a person he truly loved?

He came away from that day clear that Doug was his soulmate and, that he would do everything in his power to not destroy his wife. When it came time to share his decision with his wife, John spoke from his heart and laid it all out - and then what they did made all the difference. Initially, John allowed the time

Hearts do not lie,
minds will to
protect us.

for his wife to absorb this information, followed by allowing more time to work through their fears and transition their relationship **together**. They had a love for each other that went beyond them, and they tapped into this universal love to guide them through this journey. To this day, the source of their relationship has never changed because their love for each other was and is bigger than attachment. Their love is unconditional.

When our decisions come from a place of love for ourselves and others, and not fear, we empower our personal growth and provide an opportunity for others to grow as well. Unfortunately, fear is a constant friend and teacher, so it will return to haunt us in another form at some point and loving ourselves enough to move through it allows us to release and grow. The more we learn to do this, the less time it will take us to acknowledge fear and move past it whenever it rears its ugly head.

Loving ourselves creates a larger capacity to love others. By loving ourselves first, we make decisions that benefit both ourselves and others because our self love allows us to hold a healthy love for everyone else.

3. To love is to serve, but not at the expense of our own selves.

There is something devotional about love. It has a giving, serving quality to it which is part of what makes it so special. However, many of us forget ourselves in love and that we are also one of the recipients in the giving portion of the love equation. Not only do we not turn our own love inward, love ourselves first, be gentle with ourselves first - we also create further difficulties by putting up walls, creating defense mechanisms to not let another person's love in - all in the name of not wanting to be hurt or deal with our own issues from the past. These behaviors encourage us to focus on loving others, giving to others, without checking in on our own needs.

The following is an explanation by Joe Martino, one of the founders of Collective Evolution, on the qualities of unhealthy love versus healthy love.

"Unhealthy love can be seen as giving up aspects of yourself simply to please someone that you might be with. It can also come when you depend on the other person or need them for your own happiness or joy. Unhealthy love can be addictive and keep you locked up in stagnant periods of life where you use this form of love to avoid moving past your own challenges. Simply, unhealthy love is more about what the mind's idea of love is. It can often involve playing games, manipulation, sacrifice and so on, all of which you will notice is quite draining to do, yet you can't let it go."

"Healthy love," he continues, "is something that is mutual between two people and no one gives themselves up to experience it. It is based on a feeling within versus what's going on on the outside. It's about allowing your partner to go through their own experiences and not judge them. Support them and understand them regardless of if they may have triggered a button within you. Together, you are open, can communicate and grow. You don't need each other but simply work as a team to move through life."

Not coming from a place of need is crucial to establish a healthly love connection because when our relationships are based on need, whether we need someone, or someone needs us, we are not without judgment. Every dynamic in the relationship then either becomes about judging how we are being treated by that person we need or judging that person who needs us.

The point is we have the power to choose how our story, our life is going to unfold. No matter how much we are a serving, loving person - it should never be at the expense of our own happiness. If we focus on making sure we are giving ourselves the love we need - through self care, through allowing ourselves to follow our own passions - loving the other people in our lives will naturally fall into a healthy place. It falls into a healthy place because when we love ourselves, we have more love to give and more than that, we want to give it from a pure place within us without judgment.

Love gives us the strength and courage to grow. And growing in love brings us closer and closer to who we are meant to be, as well as allows us to show up for what we are meant to live.

PART SEVEN

Grow in love.

"*The beginning of love is the will to let those we love be perfectly themselves, the resolution not to twist them to fit our own image. If in loving them we do not love what they are, but only their potential likeness to ourselves, then we do not love them: we only love the reflection of ourselves we find in them.*"

~ Thomas Merton, No Man Is An Island

My year off turns out to be a very necessary year of self re-discovery. It is filled with incredible highs and soul-searching lows. Leaving the business behind opened a lot of space up to examine everything about myself, and my relationships, that I love or want to change. To make the opportunity to see the world in this light, with a clear and peaceful mind, is something I wish for everyone on this planet.

The biggest realization I experience in this time of reflection is to focus on being present in my life and not feel like I am wasting time or falling behind on my dreams. To help me achieve this new way of being, I create a measurement of time that is not in minutes, hours, or days, and not by appointments. It is in simple units of happiness. That's right, units of happiness now help me to fully appreciate my life in moments. It is much less overwhelming, and much more enjoyable to experience my life for the constant precious gifts that it reveals, than to focus on the mistakes of the past or the things that have not yet happened.

Now this doesn't mean I only live in a happy state and every day is roses and rainbows. What it does mean is I live in a state of gratitude as much as I can, which helps me to remain present and focused in my life and prepares me to deal with the inevitable life changes that appear along the way. It creates space for moments like this next one to rise to the surface as a necessary part of my journey to be the person I am meant to be in this world.

It's 2009, three years after our year off, and I am not a happy camper. I feel a tremendous amount of guilt for it too - as I am smack in the middle of running my second successful business with Isabelle; traveling twelve weeks a year; a solid network of authentic friends and family surround me; and we own a beautiful home in one of the best cities in the world - Vancouver, British Columbia.

Even though I am going through the actions of living this wonderful life, my heart feels like I can contribute so much more to the world. This feeling creates a core belief that I am living inauthentically. Although I authentically love the people in my life and support them with my whole heart - it is how I am treating myself and not respecting my needs that feels unfulfilling. I am not listening to my heart and what it's saying about my true path in life. Essentially, the big reason why I am here on this earth - my purpose.

Isabelle and I have worked together most of our relationship, and to share that our life's work is not fulfilling me, and have the conversation focus completely and utterly on my needs - is a huge bucket of fear that I need to lift and dunk over my head in one fell swoop. I have spent years building not one, but two businesses with Isabelle, and all of it with an immense love for my partner and the motivation of having fun being creative. But this need that I now hear calling from the pit of my soul can be ignored no longer.

In running both of our businesses, Isabelle and I have always sought out the help and guidance of a business coach. Having that third party available to help us through our growth challenges, whether personally or professionally, is very effective for us - especially because we both live and work together.

It's in one of our sessions with our coach that my proverbial fear bucket is dumped. Her intuition picks up that something is weighing on me and weighing on me big, so I am not naive to the fact that she skillfully guides our session that day to make me feel safe enough to open my heart and speak.

"I'm not happy," I finally say. "I am no longer having fun doing this."

There, I opened the floodgates and the rest of how I am feeling about the call to follow my purpose comes pouring out. Isabelle listens to me intently, all the while her big, beautiful blue eyes never leaving my face. I want so much for her to understand that this conversation has nothing to do with my love for her or her making me unhappy. If I was miserable in a job at another company and wanted to leave it, it would make things a little easier to discuss today because there wouldn't be that personal connection. Our lives are so intertwined that I fear she will take things personally.

Thankfully with our coach's help, I successfully share what is in my heart, and Isabelle is successfully able to get answers to her questions. The only question I can't answer for her as she lovingly asks me is, "What do you want to do if this isn't it?"

"I don't know," is the only reply I have right now.

I have no idea what my purpose or my calling is at this point, all I know is that I need to spend some time figuring it out. Isabelle supports me in this discovery with a love that simply blows me away. Once again, she manages to surprise me. This time not only with her dedication to our relationship, but also with her dedication to my personal happiness.

For the next several months we begin to eliminate and delegate many of the tasks on my plate to create space for me away from the business to explore what it is exactly that sparks me.

Many years ago, a client gave me a book that she believed I would love. I was thrilled to receive it and looked forward to reading it, but even with these intentions for some reason it just sat on my bookshelf gathering dust for years. Until today, the day I decide it is time to embark on the journey in that book, *The Artist's Way* by Julia Cameron, to help me discover my true purpose - or heck, at least give me a clue!

In a nutshell, the process in the book begins with a three-month commitment to journaling three pages every day. It doesn't matter what I write about, it can be stream of consciousness like it can be my thoughts on a topic or event. In addition to the journaling, Julia then guides me through several exercises and tools within the book. It's the 2010 Winter Olympics in Vancouver as I am going through this process. There are parties and celebrations literally on the streets outside my home, but I persevere and am concretely dedicated to writing my three pages daily. Even while sitting in my friends' beautiful home in Mexico on vacation, I write these pages before allowing myself to play. And it is worth every page.

Every day I feel closer and closer to finding me. I become less tired, and more inspired. I have a joy for life, a spark that has been dulled for what feels like such a long time. Colors look brighter, people seem happier, I am seeing my life through a whole new lens.

With this process I begin an exploration of reconnecting with the things that I am passionate about, and slowly but surely my spark begins to burn stronger and stronger. Supported by friends and family, I become clear that there are two things that truly connect me to myself and this big world. These two things are writing and horses - and above all else - using these passions to share with people the universal love that surrounds everyone in everyday life.

The idea of spreading this incredibly positive emotion of unconditional love excites me, as I believe it can bring some significant good in today's world. So, I start up a blog called Love Matters as a way of beginning this movement, one post at a time.

When I first start writing for Love Matters I cannot believe I am putting my own voice out there to be criticized and judged. But, the message of love and all its benefits is so important to me that I place my fears of criticism and judgment on the back-burner. Through pursuing my passion, my purpose, I find a beautiful community of like-minded people who also believe in the power of love to transform our world from a current state of consumption and social media to a world of experiences, connections, and intimacy - actual relationships. Returning people to focus on what's in their heart, what fulfills them, and not on how the latest cell phone or car will make them so much happier. This larger sense of connection and contribution only drives me to continue pursuing being a love messenger of sorts - and I forge on writing posts and begin spending time every week with horses to fuel my own heart and creativity, keeping me connected to what's important to me.

Having Isabelle, my partner in life, wholeheartedly support me through this journey provides me with the space, security, and freedom to really explore my life and focus on what my next step towards fulfillment looks like. A true gift of love that I will be grateful for until my last breath.

A few years later I am in the position to offer her this same gift. We are now the beginning of 2014 and Isabelle needs a serious change from the monotony that her everyday life has become. She is easily the most focused, disciplined, intense, and dedicated person I know, and so when she says she needs a change, the woman NEEDS a change. Isabelle has an insatiable passion for learning. She loves to balance the mental intensity she deals out week after week with some physical intensity as well - she requires this equilibrium to perform at her best. In addition to going to the gym three times a week, Isabelle is also an avid yogi, so she decides at this point that it's time for her to get out of her head, slow down and join a yoga teacher training program in Nicaragua to shift things up.

I have now been with Isabelle, day in and day out, for 23 years - and for 23 years I have done my best to keep up with this lady even though we can easily be compared to the turtle and the hare. She has a fire for life, and that fire is fueled by an endless amount of energy - trust me. I have way better knowledge of her rear end, than she of mine, simply because when we walk anywhere together I am always behind her! I'm exhausted. So, when Isabelle says to me, "I need to slow down for a bit," I immediately jump on that bandwagon and support her all the way.

I accompany Isabelle to Nicaragua for about a month and a half to support her in her teacher training program. I also take care of our business remotely so that she may detach from the "business world" she is so intricately intertwined with - even if for that brief time.

The day she is to teach her first "closed to the public" yoga class with her fellow yogi-mates I make sure to show up and secretly watch her from outside the studio. I am so proud of her for so many reasons and message her right afterwards to congratulate her and let her know I passed by to see her in action.

And that's the point right there. Because our love for each other exists on many levels we are constantly supporting and encouraging each other to be the best versions of ourselves.

Even as I sit in Bali writing the first draft of this book - Isabelle is here to support me, my writing, and the inevitable transformation it is bringing.

ove feels like we're expanding, not retracting. To be in a state of love is to support our own growth and to support the growth of the people around us.

My journey of self re-discovery is a launch pad for showing up in my own life. This experience brings me a few lessons I will share here. Love is growing into who we are meant to be, ask for what we need and support where it is needed, and finally, love feels like freedom.

1. Love is growing into who we are meant to be.

If we want to grow in relationships of any kind, being capable of self love is half the battle. The more self love and self care we possess, the more secure we feel to try new things or expand our comfort zones - which allows us to grow. The other half of the battle is being capable of selfless love - putting the needs of someone else first - which allows them to grow. When a relationship blossoms, learning to create a mutual healthy balance of love and support for each to grow, helps to push limits and release triggers that are hindering development.

Focusing on who and what we love in this world instead of on who and what we don't is crucial to growth. As simple as this sounds, the more we can remain positive and in gratitude, the easier it becomes to believe we can live our dreams. The same applies for the people we love. Positively supporting and loving the people who matter in our lives through their transitions helps them to believe they can live their dreams as well. Allowing them the freedom to be themselves is key. The more we support our partners, family, and friends - the more we can remain strong and positive for them when they waiver in uncertainty - and the more successful they will be at reaching that next level in their lives.

In romantic relationships, more than any other type, meeting each other half way is very important. This strategy helps both parties feel like they can do what each needs to do individually to grow, and therefore grow as a couple as a result. An example is how Isabelle and I take turns pursuing what is important to our individual journeys. It's a delicate balance between standing up for ourselves and sharing in what we each need. Showing understanding to our partner while supporting them with love, as well as personal fulfillment. This kind of flow creates a healthy love that sponsors growth and development.

The thing to remember here is we are all on this planet to help each other realize our purpose. We were not born to come out hindering others. Holding a perspective of loving and supporting ourselves and others creates many added benefits of receiving love, kindness, and generosity in return. And more than any other benefit, it fuels our own happiness.

2. Ask for what we need and support where it is needed.

Love between two people is a two-way street of giving compassion and receiving understanding - in other words seeing each other through the lens of love. If the same person is always supporting the other to learn and grow, eventually that supporting person will become resentful because they will feel like they do not have room for themselves to expand in the relationship.

Seeing each other through love means both parties coming from a place of compassion and understanding and being genuine in their support. It allows egos to take a break and helps both people in the relationship to really feel seen.

I mentioned earlier that Isabelle and I have always had a business coach for that third person perspective to help us with our challenges personally and professionally. We also believe in this form of support because it allows us to continually grow together. We are both constantly engaged in moving past our fears, limitations, and blocks. We are also constantly engaged in helping each other on this journey. All this combined creates a symbiotic growth in our relationship, one that keeps us moving along side each other no matter the path.

Letting go of what no longer serves us, or what no longer helps us to be the best version of ourselves, is also a big part of moving forward individually and together. Although letting go sounds relatively easy, it can be one of the hardest things to do because often we are letting go of habits, beliefs, or attitudes that have been ingrained into our system for a very long time. Things

The thing to
remember here is we are
all on this planet to
help each other realize
our purpose.

like guilt, worry, and stress are also added "baggage" that never brings us any good and only takes up precious time, space and presence.

3. Love feels like freedom.

Positive thoughts and words can create some of the most powerful energy in the Universe. So can love. Dr. Masaru Emoto, a Japanese author and entrepreneur who claimed that human consciousness influences the molecular structure of water, performed an experiment to study the impact of positivity.

"It was 1994," he said, "when the idea to freeze water and observe it with microscope came upon me. With this method, I was convinced that I should be able to see something like snow crystals. After two months of trial and error, this idea bore fruit. The beautifully shining hexagonal crystals were created from the invisible world. My staff at the laboratory and I were absorbed in it and began to do many researches. At first, we strenuously observed crystals of tap water, river water, and lake water. From the tap water we could not get any beautiful crystals. We could not get any beautiful ones from rivers and lakes near big cities, either. However, from the water from rivers and lakes where water is kept pristine from development, we could observe beautiful crystals with each one having its own uniqueness."

Dr. Emoto and his team then observed distilled water (pure water) in four ways. They observed the crystals of frozen water after showing words to the water, showing pictures to the water, playing music to the water, and finally praying to the water.

"The result was that we always observed beautiful crystals after giving good words, playing good music, and showing, playing, or offering pure prayer to water," says Dr. Emoto. "On the other hand, we observed disfigured crystals in the opposite situation. Moreover, we never observed identical crystals."

Dr. Masaru Emoto's experiments show that positive words, pictures, music, and speech hold enough positive energy to shift matter. Imagine what positive thoughts and attitudes could shift within us and others.

To feel the positivity and freedom of love is to feel lightness and joy. Whether in a relationship for 10 weeks or 10 years, surrendering to love allows us to experience life fully. In new relationships, this is called the honeymoon phase, in long-term relationships this is called necessary.

John Ashley-Pryce and Doug Stimson are two courageous men introduced earlier in this book. They have been together since 1980 and have lived and loved through many trials and tribulations. When asked what keeps their love alive after so many years, here is their advice:

1. Always respect and look after each other.
2. Sharing the same values is key.
3. Love requires compromise, moving in the same direction together, and open communication.
4. Knowing when NOT to say something is very important. Let it go and it passes, joy returns, and that's all that matters.
5. BE together. Explore, play, learn, and grow...together.

When new relationships surrender to love, essentially, we are enabling togetherness and diving into something bigger than ourselves. It is a place of discovery as everything is new. A place where the mundane day-to-day events do not matter. In this moment, we are completely and utterly focused on the feeling of oneness with another person.

To surrender to love when we have known a person for many years, is to discover at greater depths. To continue to build on the foundation that was created many years ago. To build a space with our partner that allows us to become aware of the love within each other and for each other, and then to open to the universal love that exists. This access to the feeling of something bigger than the both of us, encourages us to continue to grow and soar to the next phase of life together. The main reason some long-term relationships end up in a place of feeling out of love, is because we have stopped building on that foundation and digging deeper. The discovery has come to a halt.

The world deserves to experience love and the special gifts each of us have to offer. Believing in ourselves and supporting our partners becomes crucial to our continued pursuit of life. Once we are on this path, working through the anchors of our past - whatever they may be - really launches us towards freedom.

PART EIGHT

Live your own life.

"*The act of forgiveness takes place in
our own mind. It really has nothing to do with
the other person. The reality of true forgiveness
lies in setting ourselves free from holding
on to the pain. It's simply an act of releasing
ourselves from the negative energy.*"

~ Louise Hay

can honestly admit I try to live and breathe love with every word I say and every action I take. Most of it comes naturally, some of it I must consciously make the decision to respond with love because I know in the end, it is the right thing to do. It is what I can stand by.

I am only human though and do have my moments. Trust me. One of these moments bestows itself upon me in 2011. I am rushed into emergency surgery one summer evening while attending Isabelle's very large family reunion in her hometown of Lac Megantic, Quebec. I am taken to the very hospital where Isabelle was born, and it blows my mind to realize this is happening. They tell me I have an oversized and painful abscess that needs to be drained as it is on the verge of exploding in my body. It makes me feel lucky despite my misfortune as they compare my abscess to a ticking time bomb. It does not feel good at all.

Days later I am at home in Vancouver, painfully recuperating and contemplating not only my sore body, but my sore ego as well. I can barely move, and in addition to that I have the embarassing memory of getting escorted off a very full airplane because I needed a doctor's note to say I am safe to fly after surgery, and didn't have it. Not an ideal situation for an introvert to be in, having an airplane full of people stare you down as you make each and every one of them late for their next "thing". I can't help but feel quite miserable, frustrated, vulnerable, and worst of all, I feel so sorry for myself. If I knew now that four months down the road I will require two more surgeries, an even more painful recovery period with an at-home nurse, and will also be closely followed by a specialist for the next two years to resolve the problem – I might lighten up.

The worse part is I'm not quite sure what is putting me in this state. Is it my lack of normal ability? The pain? The fact that there are certain things I simply cannot do for myself right now and need to surrender to be taken care of? Me, the ultimate nurterer? Maybe, but all I feel at this moment is there isn't enough love in the world to get me to even crack a smile, let alone fill my heart with joy.

I know I have so much to be grateful for, tons of love surrounding me...and Isabelle. The woman that I have spent so many years of my life loving so willingly. The woman who is doing everything needed to take care of me because she loves me that much. Usually all I need to do to turn myself around in times like these is tap into the love within, connect to my higher power, express my gratitude, and spread some of that love to my loved ones and the people around me through my writing. That always feels great and fills my heart with good instantly.

Well, on this day what usually works for me simply doesn't. I fill my heart and extend love to others, and then instantly I return to a state of funk. Part of me thinks, "Oh Maggie, suck it up will ya?" but I cannot care less.

I lie there for quite some time wondering where to go next, and then in a moment of silence, solitude, and me and my words, it comes to me. I decide to make a second attempt and write a blog post on Love Matters. Yes, it starts off as a rant of a blog post, but this rant leads me to a very valid realization - once again, a little self love is missing from my life. Allowing myself the time to process what has happened in the past week by indulging in self pity and expressing my anger around neglecting my well being is what I need right now to release my current state of discontent. Most of all, feeling these emotions lead me to forgiving myself for not taking care of me.

According to Louise Hay, an American motivational author, abscesses are a manifestation of suppressed anger and one of the techniques to begin releasing this anger is forgiving ourselves.

I was brought up by beautiful givers, and this created a very nurturing, selfless behavior in me – which I cherish deeply. It also however, provides me with constant challenges in my life that are teaching me to love myself first so that I have what it takes to give to others.

I'm a Virgo. I have high expectations, am hard on myself, and can serve people 'til the cows come home - and this sense of servitude often promotes self neglect and enables me to easily place others first. I didn't realize until I developed the abscess that I carry some anger around this piece in my life. As much as I enjoy nurturing others, a part of me sees my nurturing as a weakness and not having the courage to love myself and help myself face my own demons.

Forgiving myself for not placing myself first enough in my life is the next step to healing, and it is a process. One that I have never been closer to moving through because I can see now how my world, my life and thus me, opens right up every time I do forgive and offer myself my own love.

As I continue to forgive myself as new things arise, it becomes easier to forgive others in my life. I discover that it is possible to forgive and let go. It is possible for me because the more self awareness I gain and the more clarity I get on how the events of my life have affected me so far, the more I am able to begin to release what no longer serves me. It took my abscess to shed some light on what I didn't realize was within me.

I am always amazed by the journey I need to take when it comes to thinking of my needs. Every time I find myself in this frustrating position it is like a slap in the face. The beauty in being aware of this side of myself now, is that I can wholeheartedly say that this journey gets shorter and shorter every time. Forgiveness is a continuous process, and a journey that is tightly woven with gratitude. No one is perfect, and forgiveness is the ability to realize that and move forward with love. Also, as we are constantly falling into old patterns of behavior, the future becomes about how quickly we can identify an old pattern and then change it.

To share the strength and message in unconditional love, and help others shift from getting out of their heads and into their hearts, is why I live. What I constantly need to remind myself of is that it is okay for me to be vulnerable and lean on that love occasionally.

I lived in Isabelle's shadow for years, mostly my own doing. Too much fear of showing up and being me, and then ultimately being rejected. I also got lost in servitude, making sure my loved ones were happy and feeling supported because that is what I know. Hiding out, unknowingly holding myself back, and often forgetting about my needs, is not allowing me to reach a level of happiness that following a true purpose brings.

One of the main reasons I am writing this book is to hopefully help others by triggering some insights and by increasing awareness through my own experiences. If anything I have lived through and discuss here can help another soul, I am grateful.

This part of the book holds many major shifts for me and some beautiful insights. What I will share more with you now is how love cannot grow without forgiveness, the importance of loving ourselves first so we can give, and realize that everyone has their own journey to fulfill.

1. Love cannot grow without forgiveness.

Louise Hay has stood out for me front and center in writing this chapter. I love how she sees forgiveness as she shares, "Forgiveness is a gift to yourself. It frees you from the past, past experiences, and past relationships. It allows you to live in the present time. When you forgive yourself and forgive others, you are indeed free. There is a tremendous sense of freedom that comes with forgiveness. Often you need to forgive yourself for putting up with painful experiences and not loving yourself enough to move away from those experiences. So love yourself, forgive yourself, forgive others and be in the moment. See the old bitterness and the old pain just roll off your shoulders as you let go, and the doors of your heart open wide. When you come from a space of love you are always safe. Forgive everyone. Forgive yourself. Forgive all past experiences. You are free."

Making mistakes is being human. Perfection does not exist, and I've learned this the hard way by striving to be a perfectionist. Any attempt to consistently strive for it is futile, and I believe the definition of insanity. The more we strive for perfection, the harder we will fall every time. If we can learn to forgive ourselves for making mistakes, then we have a chance at accepting what is, without fear, and marching on.

While writing this book in Bali, I visit a sacred water temple. Under a fountainhead in this temple I am given the opportunity to let go of something that is no longer serving me. Without hesitation, I release perfectionism. I choose this because

Making mistakes
is being human.

I know only too well the tight grip of perfection...and I can no longer tolerate that hold on me. By giving myself permission to let go of it, I immediately start my journey to accepting my mistakes. And what I quickly discover is that dealing with my occasional shortcomings takes way less energy than carrying around the weight of perfectionism.

Ultimately, in every challenge we experience there is something we need to learn. Every argument, every frustration, every trigger we may have all lead to teaching us something we have not yet mastered.

2. Love ourselves first so we can give.

I want to share something I lovingly created and read to myself without fail every day during my journey of integrating Cameron's *The Artist's Way* into my life. I have not read it since that journey and feeling very fortunate to reconnect with it now. These tiny daily reminders are so important to keeping us on track. This is my artist's prayer.

Universe, open your arms
And I promise to see
The opportunity, love, and abundance
that awaits me
Help me be patient with myself
Love myself and nurture myself

I am a vessel for your creativity
I trust that I am worthy
and that your guidance will
lead me, down my own divine path
Heal me thru loving myself, loving others
And accepting others love of me

~~~~~~

Being brave, owning our stories, and loving ourselves no matter what - are three things we need to embrace to forgive ourselves. If we can't forgive ourselves and love who we are, how do we expect others to do the same? It all starts with numero uno.

Easier said than done, I know, trust me. However, no matter how big we think our capacity to love is right now, it becomes monumental once we embrace self love. The reason being when we choose to love ourselves, we are not only taking care of ourselves, but also filling our reservoirs to give. What happens when we don't give love to ourselves is eventually we run out, and we rely on other people to give us love to refuel - which defies the very nature of self love and creates an unfair expectation of others. Not only do we suffer when that happens, but others do as well because we have nothing left to give them in return.

When we take the time and space to refuel ourselves with love, then give love to others, and then fill up on love again - we create a constant flow of healthy love that nurtures everyone, including ourselves. Feeling happy in our own love first is key, everything else is a bonus.

Another beautiful thing about this cycle is the more we give love, the more it returns to us. Something to remember however, is that it may not return to us from the same place or person we give it to - but trust that it will show up. It always does.

3. Realize that everyone has their own journey to fulfill.

We have all been put on this earth to fulfill a piece of a much larger puzzle. Everyone has their own path in life to follow to complete their piece. Even if the goals are similar, each piece will be different because each person is different. We are all unique and each have our own set of wins and challenges, gifts and fears. What is blissful for one can be a nightmare for another.

And if this is the case, judgment has no place here as we don't know what it's like to be in anyone else's shoes but our own. Judgment, that is a big word. Often used, often misguided. The more self love we carry with us, the more we can see beyond the opinions of others. Even if those opinions hurt us and trigger our defenses, because most of the time harmful opinions reflect the fear in the person giving the opinion.

In the end however, every situation happens for a reason and provides an opportunity to learn and grow. For everyone involved. We may not always recognize it at the time, and it may be revealed in the next minute, or the next 10 years - but no matter how stupid, insignificant, or ignorant something may seem, there is a reason to the madness.

I just experienced this recently as I am writing this book. I posted the quote from the beginning of Part Seven on social media as my inspiration for writing that day. It is a piece from Thomas Merton's *No Man Is An Island.* "The beginning of love is the will to let those we love be perfectly themselves, the resolution not to twist them to fit our own image. If in loving them we do not love what they are, but only their potential likeness to ourselves, then we do not love them: we only love the reflection of ourselves we find in them."

My close circle of family and friends all know me and support the direction of thought by liking the post and commenting words of encouragement because they know the significance of this message and my journey with the book.

Five minutes before my private session with my writing coach that day, an acquaintance that I barely stay in touch with writes a trivial comment that completely throws me off-track. Even though I shouldn't care about what was written, deep down I just do. Way too much.

So, with this thought burning a hole at the forefront of my mind, my coach and I begin our session. Before I can stop it, I begin to tell her that originally, I was going to discuss chapter format with her, but instead I now need to bring up something that feels somewhat off topic yet disturbs me to the core.

I launch into the social media incident and secretly cannot believe I am even sharing this with her. She waits until I am done and then stares at me with a questioning look.

"What?" I ask quite imposingly.

She finally asks, "Do you trust me to take you on a journey of exploration?"

"Ummm...yes...," I hesitantly say with a question mark clearly on my face.

She then starts to ask me a series of questions based on the physical behavior I exhibited during the time I shared the incident with her. Apparently, I showed signs of accessing information from my past when talking about this trigger. The intricate process she guides me through enables me to access memories from my childhood - memories I'm still not sure how I was able to retrieve or why this event even triggered them, but it does. When we're done the process, I reach a fundamental clarity about why I am built the way I am today like never before.

I instantly realize it doesn't matter what that acquaintance actually said on social media, what matters is what it triggered. I have already been given my reason for why it happened, that day in my coaching session. And that clarity is worth more to me than any hurt from a haphazard comment - in fact I am and will remain grateful for it always.

This event teaches me that instead of sinking into a well of speculation when triggered, recognize it first as our buttons being pushed. Then trust that the reason why our buttons are being pushed will reveal itself and we will be provided the opportunity to learn and grow. We won't always know why some people say the things they say or act the way they do, but when we come from a place of love for ourselves, the world becomes a less scary place.

Love is bigger than you or me or any single one of us. It lives within all of us and ties us together, and we may be surprised what we end up learning when we keep our heart open to receiving the lessons.

PART NINE

Love without conditions.

"When you go out into the woods and you look at
trees, you see all these different trees. And some of them
are bent, and some of them are straight, and some of
them are evergreens, and some of them are whatever.
And you look at the tree and you allow it.
You appreciate it. You see why it is the way it is. You
sort of understand that it didn't get enough light, and
so it turned that way. And you don't get all emotional
about it. You just allow it. You appreciate the tree. The
minute you get near humans, you lose all that.
And you are constantly saying "You're too this, or I'm
too this." That judging mind comes in. And so I practice
turning people into trees. Which means appreciating
them just the way they are."

~ Ram Dass

t's a very gray Vancouver day and I feel about just as drab. So, I decide to get some fresh air, along with hopefully a new attitude, and bring Pixel my 18-pound, 10-year old Sheltie with me. If you don't know what kind of dog a Sheltie is, maybe this will help you out, "OMG, it's a mini Lassie!"

We hear this same exclamation from strangers worldwide every day, on every walk. Some people even venture to call for him as Lassie, and then wonder why he never engages with them. Pixel is smart, and I trust his instinct completely.

He's a very independent dog but has an uncanny intuition to purposefully share space with you when he feels sadness. On this rainy day, he can feel I am not in the best of spirits and so he takes me for a walk in our neighborhood. Literally. This may sound weird, but in that moment as my dog is pulling me around on the end of his leash, I feel he is connecting with my unhappiness - and furthermore understands that I need to shed it.

We make our way to the seawall and even though it's

raining and cold, Pixel is happy...and excited. Now, you need to know that for my dog excited usually comes with a sidedish of constant, loud, and high-pitched barking.

Well, I am not going to have any of that, especially today, so I turn to my little happy dog and tell him in a very stern voice, "Pixel, quiet happy...please!"

And, without missing a beat Pixel continues to walk with a bounce in his step, a wagging tail, a smile on his face, and wait for it.........NO BARKING. I am floored. So, on our walk we go.

He picks up a stick and prances with pride as he continues to guide me further down the seawall and won't stop until he figures I have walked out and left behind my frustrations and gloominess of the day. Throughout the walk, I try several times to turn around and go back home, fed up with my day, my attitude, myself, "Come on Pixel, let's go home!"

But every ounce of his 18 pounds and every cell of herding instinct he owns keeps on pulling me ahead, and he is usually a very obedient dog. So reluctantly, I go with it. Not one peep escapes his mouth the entire walk, he even shares a moment with me at the end of a pier as we both watch the ferries, yachts, and rowers go by. In this moment I feel a shift start to happen within me, from misery to hope. And as I stand there in this serenity with my dog, I whisper "Thank you Pixel."

My little dog is giving me hope, on a day that feels like it wants to swallow me from head to toe. I return home in a completely different state of being thanks to him. Even though we are both soaked through to the bone from the rain, I hold a much lighter, more grateful attitude that makes everything going on seem almost trivial.

As I look down at my very happy, very wet dog, I realize Pixel has a gift for reminding me about the bigger purpose of why we are here. One little 18-pound dog has that power. Proof that no matter our size, our looks, or our language, if we hold love within us it provides us and the beings around us a powerful energy that heals.

Pixel also teaches me presence and forgiveness. When we had our graphic design studio, he would come to the office with us every day and perform his role as the team mascot. It didn't matter if we were there for four hours or 14 hours, he lived every minute like it was brand new. So present. The same occurs when we leave him at home, it doesn't matter the amount of time we're away because the greeting we receive upon opening the door is always the same. He is so present that forgiveness is a non-issue because whatever has happened in the past, stays there. The focus is on the reunion and not the fact that we were gone. Now, our cat...that's a story for another time.

Three and a half years after the remarkable day in the rain, Pixel passes away. Up until his last few weeks on this planet, people always ask, "Ohhh, how old is your puppy?" every time we venture out of the house or meet someone new. A true testament to his spirit. Pixel passes away at 14 years of age which equals about 72 human years, and we wonder what gave him his youth for so long? Was it his raw diet? The fresh air of Vancouver? Sure, they can contribute, however, deep in my heart I know without a doubt what gave him his young heart and happy body. It was unconditional love.

I can easily say that what I know about unconditional love I learned from Pixel. He gave unconditional love every minute of his life. It filled his 18-pound little body with so much spirit and happiness that just being near him shifted our state of being. He had a butt and tail that wiggled feverishly to express his happiness. Whether it was seeing someone that he hadn't seen in a day or a year, going to the beach at low tide, or bumping into one of his favorite doggy friends on the street - his wiggle and his enthusiastic bark always greeted with big spirit. He effortlessly put smiles on faces every time we went outside - no matter what the person looked like, he loved them up like a rock star.

The insane amount of love this little dog could spread effortlessly wherever he roamed was a gift to anyone who met him. I saw him change the course of someone's day with a high five, turn a face of fear into pure joy on a child as he licked her nose, and snuggle up to a person who uses the sidewalk for a bed. One of our favorite things to do together was connect with the homeless people in our neighborhood who needed love. Pixel would greet them with butt wiggling and loving little nibbles and he would manage every time to pull this person out of their reality, their misery, for the time they were together. It was so beautiful and inspiring to watch how well he mastered unconditional love.

People turn to depression, anger, or hate for far less than what Pixel took in stride every day. In his last year of life, he was on four different medications for grand mal seizures, an immune deficiency disorder, urinary tract infections, and skin lesions - all of which created a variety of side effects. Not once did he ever misbehave, act out, or reduce the insane amount of love he delivered on a continual basis.

He had a knowledge of life in 14 years, that most people never acquire in an average lifetime. Sometimes I think he had a sixth sense the way he could read people, but really it was that he spoke the universal language of love. He understood people at an instinctual level.

I remember one day we were yet again on another dog walk and instead of taking our regular path, he insisted on pulling me off course - where he proceeded to lead me to reunite with my high school English and music teacher from Quebec. Unbeknownst to me, she now lived in Vancouver and reuniting with her was wonderful. She remembered me for my written compositions as a teenager and connecting with her, at a time when I was wanting to write my own book, gave me the extra courage I was lacking.

Thank you, Pixel.

Love is the best medicine. A well-known phrase that means so much. When we embrace love into our being, our soul, it does the body good. As Dr. Emoto's experiments proved, positive emotion brings on positive results.

In the following I will discuss conditional love versus unconditional love, how we need to fully experience emotions to release them, and how trusting our instincts is a non-negotiable. Period.

1. Conditional versus Unconditional Love.

In Part Six, I quote Joe Martino explaining the qualities of two types of love, unhealthy love and healthy love. Here, I want to share his thoughts on the two most typical definitions of love. Mr. Martino says, "Generally we hear love defined as either conditional or unconditional. Conditional love would be loving something based on a certain set of conditions being met. i.e. 'I only love this person if they do this for me, if they don't, then I don't love them.'"

He continues, "Unconditional love would be more so 'regardless of your choices and the fact that they may have caused me to experience painful emotions, I still love you because I recognize the purpose of our journey.' Note, this does not mean unconditional love means sacrificing, staying in unhealthy relationships or abuse etc. It simply means the feeling of love is always there. Like a mother or father loving their child."

Unconditional love is exactly that, love with no conditions. And this is precisely the kind of love I am referring to with Pixel, and the love I wish to continue to discuss in this chapter. Sharing unconditional love is huge for me because I know the good it can do. At the heart of every person is a desire to be loved for who we are, and not judged or expected to be who we're not. Most mothers are known to hold unconditional love for their children. Because children are essentially a pure, physical extension of themselves that they care for and protect, this connection breeds loving without conditions.

Animals also love unconditionally, whether with other animals or with humans like my dog Pixel. Another example of unconditional love between animal and human is my mare Powder. I strongly believe we have a lot to learn from animals, especially horses, greatly because of their lack of ego. Powder came to me as a 20-year-old horse with Cushings disease. She was the first mare I introduced into my herd. I soon discovered her greatest asset was not her beautiful blue eyes that everyone noticed first, but her innate ability to help people connect to their inner truth and move forward with confidence. She is powerful because she knows how to connect to someone's heart, and when she is there, she loves them with absolutely no judgment or conditions. To be on the receiving end of this experience gives those people permission to feel their fears and challenges, and not think about them. A very different perspective for most, providing very different results.

Unconditional love is my guiding force - what I strive for every day in every situation with every person that crosses my path. Some days I succeed better than others, but the important thing is I keep this challenge of love alive within me daily and I never give up on it.

2. Fully experience emotions to release them.

Pixel's wiggly butt taught me to really communicate what I am feeling. The fact that his entire body convulsed with joy when he was happy, left no room for interpretation. He was speaking loud and clear without saying a word, and that allowed people to understand him and respond. In most cases, it also spread love and joy in his immediate surroundings.

Bottling up our negative emotions can be devastating. I know this for a fact. Not communicating our negative emotions can lead to actual physical manifestations - as I experienced with my abscess. Acknowledging and communicating what we feel is truly important to our emotional well-being as it creates self-alignment and strengthens human connections.

Emotions connect us and help us show up as ourselves, and the more we can communicate them the more we can release them and create space within us to allow love in. This space provides us the opportunity to fill our internal reservoirs with self love. With this reservoir filled with love we are then capable of great things. Even small acts of love can create an impact.

I remember one random day in Spring a friend of mine texted me several messages with attached photos, sending me on a surprise treasure hunt. She left a trail of love messages in my neighborhood for me to find with the clues she sent. I became extremely excited...what fun!

I found a shape of a heart in fallen cherry blossoms on the ground in a local park. Then another message written in chalk that said, "Love Matters" like my blog, on a cement perch in another park not too far away. Pixel was just as excited as I was to find these treasures! And by the time we arrived to the second destination, many others had already continued to leave their own love messages using the chalk my friend had left behind. She had created some simple fun around love for me, and several people ended up being touched by her love. A beautiful surprise on a Saturday afternoon.

3. Trusting our instincts is a non-negotiable.

Being courageous in love requires following our gut even when no one else believes. We all know what is right for us, better than anyone else, and need to trust our inner voice or knowing. Have you ever decided to do something because you *think* it's the right thing to do, but your gut *feels* differently? Have you ever realized after the fact that you made the wrong decision and going with your gut would have been so much better for you in the end? If yes, that 's what we're talking about here.

Trusting our instincts increases our internal connection to our true desires and puts us even more in tune with what is best for us. The more in tune we are, the more we can focus on creating an inner softness and not putting up walls to protect ourselves. Inner softness means living with gentleness and not letting anything harden us on the inside. No matter how painful or angry we may feel, the more we can remain soft on the inside, the less barriers we create within ourselves and with others, and the more we can love unconditionally.

I think a while of Love, and while I think,
Love is to me a world,
Sole meat and sweetest drink,
And close connecting link
Tween heaven and earth.

I only know it is, not how or why,
My greatest happiness;
However hard I try,
Not if I were to die,
Can I explain.

I fain would ask my friend how it can be,
But when the time arrives,
Then Love is more lovely
Than anything to me,
And so I'm dumb.

For if the truth were known, Love cannot speak,
But only thinks and does;
Though surely out 'twill leak
Without the help of Greek,
Or any tongue.

A man may love the truth and practise it,
Beauty he may admire,
And goodness not omit,
As much as may befit
To reverence.

But only when these three together meet,
As they always incline,
And make one soul the seat,
And favorite retreat,
Of loveliness;

When under kindred shape, like loves and hates
And a kindred nature,
Proclaim us to be mates,
Exposed to equal fates
Eternally;

And each may other help, and service do,
Drawing Love's bands more tight,
Service he ne'er shall rue
While one and one make two,
And two are one;

In such case only doth man fully prove
Fully as man can do,
What power there is in Love
His inmost soul to move
Resistlessly.

Two sturdy oaks I mean, which side by side,
Withstand the winter's storm,
And spite of wind and tide,
Grow up the meadow's pride,
For both are strong

Above they barely touch, but undermined
Down to their deepest source,
Admiring you shall find
Their roots are intertwined
Insep'rably.

— Henry David Thoreau —

If love is being held back by fear, throwing out the excuses to why it's being held back is the only answer to releasing and moving onward. Holding back any emotion is not a good idea. Holding back love only causes us future regret, and life is too short for regret. People who hold back love of any kind, somewhere deep down may feel like they don't deserve to receive it.

EVERYONE DESERVES TO RECEIVE LOVE.

Everyone. Love takes many forms. It is not always transmitted through kindness and gentleness, but it does always come from a place of kindness and gentleness. It is also shared from heart to heart, from speaking what needs to be said, from looking out for people when they do not see, and from listening when we do not hear. Letting love in grounds us so we can be free to BE who we are meant to show the world. How we choose to use the fuel of love is entirely up to us.

PART TEN

Move forward together.

"When we love, we always strive to become better than we are...when we strive to become better than we are, everything around us becomes better too."

~ Paulo Coelho

sabelle and I are constantly referred to as a "Power Couple". Successful career women who have their shit together, see the world, and know what they want. Power Couple. Funny, but that term reminds me of an experience we shared in the first few years of living in Vancouver.

A friend of a friend was working on casting for a movie, you may have heard of it? *Best in Show* released in the year 2000. It presents as a documentary of five dogs and their owners destined to show in the Mayflower Kennel Club Dog Show, held in Philadelphia. They have a scene toward the end of the movie where two female characters, played by Jane Lynch and Jennifer Coolidge, become lovers and start a magazine called *American Bitch*. They need female couples to pose with dogs for mock magazine covers in the movie. So, Isabelle and I join several other women in a day long photo shoot to create these cover pages. Once they meet all of us, they give each couple a theme that will be created for each mock cover of *American Bitch*. Two very muscular women pose for a fitness cover holding two Sheltie puppies. Another couple portrays the organic, vegan lifestyle shot carrying a Cocker Spaniel. And then there's Isabelle and I - the "Power Couple" dressed in business attire with a Dalmatian.

Because the photo shoot focuses on the upper half of our bodies, the dogs need to be held in our arms to be seen. Two Sheltie puppies? Awww no problem, so cute! A Cocker Spaniel? Still very doable and the image is of one very happy family. But a Dalmatian? Come on! Poor Isabelle takes the brunt of holding up this massive dog while I play up the camera and smile pretty. Now, the point of this story isn't to complain or indicate that I love being in front of the camera, but more the fact that these people know us from a hole in the wall and still peg us as the power couple from the start.

And that we are, still to this day there's no denying it. We both strive to learn and grow constantly. We are smart, dedicated workers that love being the drivers of our lives. We both decided long ago that children were not in our future, so our home life includes animals. Over the years we've had a dog, cats, bunnies, birds, a guinea pig, and fish! After Pixel passed away, it was the first time since we've met that we did not have one single pet. Not one! Until now.

Now, we have five horses and one barn cat, and this makes me shine with happiness. These horses are truly my partners, and they collaborate with me to help create heart-centered transformation for people through equine-facilitated learning. Together, the horses and I hold a safe space of unconditional love and trust. A place where people can be vulnerable and look inward to face their fears, challenges, obstacles and limiting beliefs without judgment. This is my heart work and I feel blessed to now incorporate this type of facilitation into our business.

Since Isabelle and I are life and business partners, time away from the business to hangout is essential. We make sure to have meals together once a day if not twice, we take an evening away from home once a week, and then we travel together several times a year mostly to visit family and friends. We call our weekly time away "Date Nights". On that night every week, we do not schedule any evening seminars or dinners with friends because Isabelle and I go out on a date, just the two of us. Sometimes we go for dinner and a movie, sometimes we see a live act, go for a walk on the beach, or try something new. The point is we share at least one evening per week as a romantic couple. No business, no interruptions - and it works. We both hold an exceptional standard of discipline and dedication at work, and we need to make sure we hold that same standard at play. Balance is so important not to burn out. Maintaining balance is also part of why Isabelle is an avid yogi and I a horse lover. Without these activities to keep our minds and our bodies at peace, we would never be able to give of ourselves in the quantity that we do.

In fact, it is on one of our more recent dates that I discovered that Isabelle was actually stalking me all those years ago when I would see her on the city bus every morning on the way to school.

"I was conducting recon!" she says.

She apparently wanted to know everything about me outside of school - where I lived, who I hung out with, and she would try to catch a glimpse of something from my life every time I came toward that bus stop. Oh, and on top of that she tells me that her liking "Paul" in the theatre department in our first semester was a decoy!

"I was never into him. It gave me a very good reason to connect with you at the time," she admits with a smile.

Point is, spending time as a couple can still be revealing after over two decades together.

What has also worked successfully with Isabelle and I as a couple and as business partners, is that we constantly question our journey together. Is it still what we both want? Are we happy? Has a part of it gone stale? Which part? Do we need to make any changes and what could those be? And so on...we aim to never take our lives and our time together for granted.

The fact that we make a point to check-in and face these tough questions regularly is a big part of why we keep growing as a couple. We both have the desire to be happy people, and as life shifts and changes we both want to help each other move to that next level.

Creating plans for our future also helps us to stay on track with what we both want individually and together. By planning together, we make sure to include the other in each of our journeys. Resulting in moments like Isabelle supporting me writing this book in Bali, and I supporting her in her yoga teacher training in Nicaragua. Creating plans together allows us to be a

Sitting in my room,
A candle burning away
the loneliness in my heart,
I think of you
and the things that you do,
That make my life a happy place.

A white, furry mound,
Held close to my chest,
A smile crosses my face,
Memories of times shared
and glimpses of future moments,
Fill my mind with happiness.

Alone, you make my world
a better place,
And together, we create
magic.

— Margarita Romano —

part of achieving our individual and mutual goals together and doing this nurtures our engagement level and our relationship.

Moving forward together takes love, time, work, commitment, and one hell of a support system. Our family and friends are so important to us, as well as our business coach and mentors. Their love, support, guidance, and most of all genuine care for our well being as individuals and as a couple - are a big part of why Isabelle and I succeed. We know we have a soft place to land without judgment, and having that feeling is priceless.

The gems I want to impart in this last section of the book are the importance of planning together, how love is reminding each other of our power and beauty when it has been forgotten, how to remain in a state of love after massive change, and always communicate from the heart.

As a couple, supporting each other in our own personal development and sharing these journeys together is crucial. The more we involve each other in our personal paths, the more the journey together has a chance at successfully shifting to fulfill both people.

1. The importance of planning together.

A lot of us fear change, mostly because it opens a big can of uncertainty. And because we fear it, our instinct is to not openly communicate about it with our partners. Sometimes to the point of not even admitting to ourselves that we need a change to happen. The thing is, the more we involve our partners in the path our heart wants to take, the more likely we will work out a way to make it happen together. Initially there may be resistance, from both parties, that is normal. The important thing is to push through and move forward together.

When I first realized I wanted to work with horses to help people transform their lives, I didn't know what to do with those thoughts. Going from being a corporate writer and owning a brand strategy business to working with horses...what???

However, I started to discuss it with Isabelle anyway because that's where change starts, by putting it out there. Admittedly in the beginning she was a little confused and not even entirely understanding how I wanted to partner with the horses. And if I'm to be completely honest I didn't quite understand it all either. I just knew I had a calling in my heart to go down this path, and I knew I didn't need to know how, just what.

The more we discussed it, the more the right people and places started to appear, and clarity took shape. The next thing we knew, we were planning together to create a retreat center where we would host private and group retreats for business owners. Isabelle would work with them on brand and business strategy, and I would help them move through the obstacles holding them back from their success through equine-facilitated learning. It was beautiful!

And with a ton of trust, patience, and persistence I can proudly say that today Isabelle and I own an equestrian estate named Trailblazers, where we hold retreats and have a beautiful herd of five horses. We managed to combine our passions to create something phenomenal by working together.

Isabelle and I don't always agree with where the other is heading initially, or sometimes it's more that we can't visualize what the other is suggesting. Patience, persistence, and peace is our solution.

1. Be patient and make sure to fully hear each other's perspective.
2. Persist through all the tough questions and discussions to work through the discomfort this change is creating for the both of you.
3. Be at peace with the decisions made and trust that if you work it together, you will grow together.

2. Love is reminding each other of our power and beauty when it has been forgotten.

If there is anything you take away from this book, let this valuable piece of information be at the top of your list: Love is reminding each other of our power and beauty when it has been forgotten. Reminding the special people in our lives that we believe in them, and sharing all the things we still see in them, goes a very long way. Often when we fear change, we doubt ourselves. For a friend,

Love is reminding each
other of our power and
beauty when it has been
forgotten.

a lover, a sibling to step in at that point and believe in us is enough to pull us through the fear - that, and faith, is irreplaceable.

Whichever goal or dream you are focusing on, helping each other to always become better, always strive for the best version of ourselves, is one of the biggest, most valuable gifts we can give each other. Love, unconditional love, always wants the best for all parties involved. And, it is this selfless love that creates and enables change.

Bill Hathaway from Yale University shares his findings on selfless love. "Romantic love tends to light up the same reward areas of the brain that are activated by cocaine. But new research shows that selfless love—a deep and genuine wish for the happiness of others—actually turns off the brain's reward centers."

The reward turns into fulfillment and gratitude from the good feelings generated from giving and helping others. Selfless love has the power to shift people - imagine what it can do for the growth of our own personal relationships.

3. How to remain in a state of love after massive change.
One single moment is all it takes for everything to change. Life hits hardest when we least expect it and dealing with the aftermath can sometimes put an irreversible strain on a relationship. The death of a loved one, a catastrophe, the end of a long-term relationship, a terminal illness, the loss of a job, house, vehicle - all these situations can create so much stress, pain, and tension

between two people that there can be a complete loss of faith and hope to ever reconnect and rebuild.

Depending on the scenario at hand, allowing the freedom to grieve is a necessary step. There is no amount of time that is the right amount to grieve. It really is about how long it takes us to go through the process. There are five stages of normal grief that were first proposed by Elisabeth Kübler-Ross in her 1969 book *On Death and Dying*. They are denial and isolation, anger, bargaining, depression, and acceptance. And until we have gone through these stages, any resistance will only extend the process of healing.

Anne Mieke Kirkby knows all too well about the five stages of grief. Only one month after giving birth to her first child did she lose her mother to a sudden death from a bacterial infection. The whole event took place within a 24-hour period and this tragedy completely sideswiped her and her family.

Still vulnerable from giving birth, Mieke quite quickly isolated herself to deal with the shock. She didn't reach out for a ton of support, she simply couldn't. Once the realization hit that her mother was gone, Mieke found herself to be very angry...and sad. She felt it was so unfair how it all happened. Unfair that her baby boy wouldn't get to grow up with his maternal grandmother. Unfair that they barely had time to say goodbye. Unfair that she was now parentless, having already lost her father at a young age.

Mieke allowed herself the time to work through all her grief and emotions. She says, "Feeling through the anger was so important and love allowed me to do that. Love is all-encompassing and all the feelings that I felt were from a state of love."

Her mother was a presence of love for her, for her entire life. This special bond allowed Mieke to connect to her heart to fully process her emotions and truly feel the grief in all its forms. Today, Mieke has found a way to keep that connection to her parents alive within her. When Mieke feels the sun on her face and heart she knows her mother's spirit is with her, and when she feels the heat of the sun on her back, it is her father. Such a beautiful way to stay connected to the kind of love only parents can provide.

Engaging in activities that fuel the soul also helps to connect us to a beautifully healing love. When coming out of the stages of grief, pursuing the things that truly move us creates an opening of the heart chakra that begins to put us back together. When we are grieving, love can feel far away, but access to it is always there. Participating in soulful activities can help re-engage us into our lives.

4. Communicate from the heart.

Author Margaret Weis says, "Words can never fully say what we want them to say, for they fumble, stammer, and break the best porcelain. The best one can hope for is to find along the way someone to share the path, content to walk in silence, for the heart communes best when it does not try to speak."

When I first read this quote the writer in me found it VERY hard to admit that words are simply not enough, until the lover in me chimed in and it all made sense. The essence of love is best shared through who we are, through our actions, through the energy we send out into the world and receive back...through what is shared in silence. Words have not a chance to compete with what the soul can share through love. This, I know. Even as a writer.

Looking at the bigger picture that holds our life path, a path that is continuously filled with shared silent moments, is so important to experiencing love at its finest. Moments like when I woke up one morning and my baby niece was quietly cuddling with me, eyes wide open yet happy to be warm and near; or when I had a bad day and my honey and my dog just sat with me to turn it right around; or even like when a horse found me in a field and nuzzled its head under my arm because it was so sorry it had just bucked me off after getting spooked. These moments are all wordless yet filled with love, and more importantly, precious to what make up our journey. Love experienced with different people and beings, in different moments...yet continuous.

I find this comforting. Comforting in that even though we are not with everyone in our lives all the time, we do regularly experience moments of the soul with each and every one of them and that's what matters.

Jean, Jean the dancing machine, Stimson is one classy lady. At 97, she is beautiful, happy, and loving life for everything that it is and surrounds herself with family and friends as much as possible. A lot of people love Jean, and to that she simply says, "Well, I love them right back!"

She believes being in a state of love is a natural thing to do – and I couldn't agree more. Being around her positivity and joy of living is contagious.

A few years ago, Isabelle asked her what insights she would now give her 40-year-old self. Here is what she shared:

1. Accept what is at present. If you can help change it for the better, do it graciously.
2. Don't be too proud to ask advice from others you trust. 'Cause you don't know what you don't know!
3. Arguing to be right at any cost is a sign of weakness and a lack of confidence.
4. We're always building up or tearing down in everything we do, so ask yourself often, "Are you on the construction or the wrecking crew?"

In the process of writing this book, sadly Jean has passed away, and her openly loving spirit is carried by family and friends daily. This woman lived in the present, took the time to have heart connections with people, and had a wit and grace about her that made everyone smile. She has taught many of us what it means to honor and respect others and she is dearly missed.

Speaking and sharing from the heart is essential for intimate human connection. When we do not communicate our truth, we can never truly be happy because we either sit with regret for not having spoken or sit with hurt or anger for not having spoken our truth. And when we do use our words to communicate, have the awareness of choosing them with care as they do make an impact - and can change a person for better or for worse.

Love matters...and when we allow our heart to shine through our words and our actions, we open a beautiful opportunity that we will be heard from same.

Love will get you there.

"*If we looked down at the world from space, we would not see any demarcations of national boundaries. We would simply see one small planet, just one.*"

~ *Dalai Lama*

Love is one of the highest vibrations in the Universe. In simple terms, what this means is because we are all made of energy, the emotion of love shifts our energy to vibrate at its highest, thus attracting other similar energy to it. This is why when we first fall in love, everything around us seems to feel great.

Everyone has what it takes to experience love. Unfortunately, we can let life get in the way of what we instinctively want to give and receive, and suddenly love can become a challenge. Over-analyzing the daily events of our lives is guaranteed to kill our happiness. Because of past traumas and hurtful experiences, we live our lives with the many filters we have created over the years through conditioning for survival. Loving ourselves, even a little, begins to set us free from the shackles of these filters. Self love lifts us up and provides us a whole new perspective – it returns us to the one that we were born with that is filter-free.

When we decide to allow ourselves the opportunity to

connect to the heart, miracles can happen. As you know, for me writing and horses bring me home. Since that time in my life years ago of journaling three pages daily to rediscover my passions in life, connecting to my heart has led me to writing this book. My first book by me. I have been a writer for years, but other than my blog, I have always written for other people - either through corporate collateral or ghostwriting. So, this piece is quite the personal journey for me and I am so grateful for every step it has encouraged me to take. Thank you for being a part of this journey as well.

As mentioned earlier, I am now also a certified equine-facilitated coach with my own herd at our beautiful equine estate on Vancouver Island. I help heart-centered business owners work through what is stopping them from owning their genius, while Isabelle works her magic at helping them deliver their genius in a simple, impactful, and differentiating way. Working with horses in this manner creates a safe space to help people rewrite the stories of their life - past and present. It helps them move forward with a loving connection to themselves, and to others, allowing people to live the life they truly want.

The finely-tuned instinct of a horse allows them to be very effective mirrors for us and reflect what we're holding inside energetically every second. Because horses are prey animals they are required to be hyper sensitive and intuitive to their environment for their survival. They need to be able to determine the difference between a hungry cougar approaching and one that's just passing by. They do this by reading the intention of the cougar in their space to know what's going on for their survival. If they fled every time something came near, they would be exhausted for when they really do need to run away.

Horses do the same with us when we are in their space. They are constantly reading us to determine our true intentions. They'll continuously read our energy to know what's going on for their survival. They also have a psychological impact on us. Because they are such large animals we need to be more present around them. This allows us to build an inner sensitivity to what's going on for us in their presence.

This powerful combination creates a very sensitive, vulnerable and safe space to facilitate a coaching experience through an equine partnership. My training allows me to interpret the horses' behaviour in the presence of whoever I bring into the space, and communicate it in a way that may trigger insight and personal discovery for them.

This kind of work feeds my soul in ways I didn't even know existed. And who knew I could experience life in this state until I took the time to ask myself, "What do I really want?"

It may seem impossible in the beginning...but just do it. Ask yourself – WHAT DO I REALLY WANT? Trust that you can get there with love - and you will.

About the author

Margarita Romano is a "super freak" processor helping heart-centered entrepreneurs connect the dots to lead spectacular lives driven by heart and soul. She has a BFA from Concordia University in Montreal and is also one of the best selling authors of the business and marketing book titled, *The Next Big Thing: Top Trends From Today's Leading Experts to Help You Dominate the New Economy*. As a certified equine-facilitated coach, she now lives on Vancouver Island at her equestrian estate Trailblazers, where she is more wildly passionate about horses than ever and may often be found hanging out with her favorite four-legged beings rain or shine.